THE DARK MERMAID

THE DARK MERMAID

By
Amar Shrestha

PILGRIMS PUBLISHING
◆ Varanasi ◆

THE DARK MERMAID

By
Amar Shrestha

Published by:
PILGRIMS PUBLISHING

An imprint of:
PILGRIMS BOOK HOUSE
(Distributors in India)
B 27/98 A-8, Nawabganj Road
Durga Kund, Varanasi-221010, India
Tel: 91-542- 2314060
Fax: 2312456
E-mail: pilgrims@satyam.net.in
Website: www.pilgrimsbooks.com

Copyright © 2008, Amar Shrestha
All Rights Reserved

ISBN: 978-81-7769-749-0

The contents of this book may not be reproduced, stored or copied in any form—printed, electronic, photocopied, or otherwise—except for excerpts used in review, without the written permission of the publisher.

Printed in India at Pilgrim Press Pvt. Ltd. Lalpur Varanasi

CONTENTS

Chapter 1.

The Gift..1

Chapter 2.

Dark as Night..8

Chapter 3.

A Curse...17

Chapter 4.

A New Beginning..24

Chapter 5.

The Pradhans..37

Chapter 6.

Stubborn Horse...46

Chapter 7.

Spitting Llama and Hitler's Telescope................60

Chapter 8.

Mount Hermon..76

Chapter 9.

Shikha and Sammy..89

Chapter 10.

The Competition..101

Chapter 11.

Learning to Breathe...110

Chapter 12.

Hoping for a Miracle..123

Chapter 13.

The Surprise..129

Chapter 14.

Fever...137

Chapter 15.

The Championships...143

Chapter 16.

A New Record...155

Chapter 17.

Neck to Neck..163

Chapter 18.

The Glory...170

CHAPTER I

THE GIFT

"Ready"… "Get set", the referee's starting pistol went off with a loud bang as he shouted, "GO!"

The eight girls, in brightly coloured swimsuits, dived into the blue waters gracefully. All that is, except for Kali, who, as usual, couldn't keep her legs straight while diving.

"Your legs, Kali, your legs," her coach had always had to point out, "Can't you keep them straight?"

For the life of her, Kali couldn't.

As they broke surface, she glanced to her left at the girl she knew was a champion in this event, the 100-metre freestyle. She had blue eyes.

"And she is so fair," thought Kali. She knew that the blue-eyed girl would be her main competitor in the event.

At twenty-five metres Kali and the blue-eyed girl were ahead of the others.

The Dark Mermaid

"But she's almost an arm's length ahead of me," she realised, and concentrated on moving her arms faster.

With this renewed effort, she made up some distance and was only half an arm's length away as they reached the end of the pool, the halfway mark. She turned for the final lap close behind the leader, but found to her dismay that the blue-eyed girl had again taken a lead of almost a metre.

"She turned really fast," the thought went through her mind, "She must have practised this many times."

Up among the rows of brightly-dressed spectators, Kali's dad shouted, "Kali, keep your chin tucked in," and, "Kali, keep your head down!"

Kali heard his shout through the cacophony of noise and couldn't stop smiling to herself, "Seems he too has learned something from watching my training day after day!"

"Kali, move your legs!" yelled her coach from the sidelines.

She heard him too, and now at the last twenty-metre mark Kali did what she was best at. Her head underwater, chin firmly tucked in, Kali started to kick with such expeditiousness that a continuous bubbly white froth began to follow her fast-kicking legs. She surged ahead with increased speed. Her

The Gift

arms, bent at right angles, scythed the water in quick efficient strokes.

Ten metres to the finish, Kali and the blue-eyed girl were level with each other. Kali's powerful legs continued to hammer the water with ferocious kicks. Now, the leader could only watch helplessly as the dark-coloured girl with the large eyes glided past her. A frothing white wake followed her.

"She's okay now," exulted her father silently, "now no one can catch up with her."

He had realised a long time ago that the secret of his daughter's speed in the water was due to the extreme quickness with which she could move her strong and muscular legs. It had not been something she had learnt during training. Instead, it had always been her God-given gift.

The one-month-long training had taught her to use her arms more efficiently, and faster, so that now Kali seemed to be unbeatable in her twelve-year-old age group.

Kali touched the finish pad, a good two arm-lengths in front of the blue-eyed girl. The crowd cheered and Kali accepted her rival's compliments graciously. She looked up and waved at her father, who was on his feet, his arms aloft in delight.

"Good show Kali," her coach pulled her out of the water, "Now you'd better go and take a rest. The backstroke starts in half an hour."

The Dark Mermaid

Kali walked back to the dressing room, the warm glow of victory enveloping her. Up in the stands, her father was shaking hands left and right, informing everyone that his daughter had won!

Half an hour later Kali was in the pool with the other contestants for the 100-metre backstroke. She again found herself beside the blue-eyed girl. Kali knew that she was competing from Lincoln's School of Kathmandu, which was the only outside school invited to participate in the Birganj City School Swimming Championships.

"She's so fair and I'm so dark," thought Kali enviously.

As the gun went off, the Lincoln girl took the lead immediately and raced ahead. For the first thirty metres Kali and the others were almost abreast of each other, while the blue-eyed girl seemed to have increased her lead. At the forty-metre mark, Kali had taken second place. She was a metre away from the leader, and half a metre ahead of the others.

The blue-eyed girl flipped over neatly at the end of the pool. However this time, Kali, just behind her, made an extra effort to turn fast herself. Forty metres to the finish, Kali had almost drawn level with the leader.

"Now, Kali, now!" yelled her coach. "Come on Kali, faster!" shouted her dad.

The Gift

Kali heard them both, even though the noise from the audience was deafening. Her legs responded at once to her command and her feet started to kick the water vigorously in a pedalling motion. The familiar frothing of the water engulfed her feet. She now moved her bent arms up and to the side in quick semicircle movements. Twenty-five metres to the finish, Kali was level with the Lincoln girl, who cast a quick worried glance at the dark girl beside her. Desperate now, she flailed at the water with her arms, her body arching with the effort. Her knees went up and down faster, but with lost rhythm.

"She's over-trying," thought Kali, "won't do her much good, that's for sure."

Kali's coach too had the same thought. He didn't have to worry about the other swimmers, who were anyway some distance behind the two leaders. However, he was aware that the Lincoln girl was good. He knew that Lincoln School had a very good coach and they prided themselves on their swimming prowess. Besides, this blue-eyed girl had been the overall champion in the Kathmandu School Championships.

"She's swimming out of rhythm," he observed, "her knees are pumping too high."

"Kali," he shouted, "take it easy. Keep your body straight. Knees underwater."

The Dark Mermaid

Kali heard him through all the screaming of the spectators and did as she was told. Her feet, all the while, continued to pedal furiously; her bent arms cut the water behind and to the sides in neat and rapid strokes.

Ten metres to the finish, Kali surged ahead of the blue-eyed girl like a shark after prey. The blue-eyed girl could only watch and admire the dark-skinned legs kick up a white bubbling froth as they passed by her.

A white wake followed Kali. As she touched the finish pad, Kali silently thanked her coaching for teaching her to swim in a straight line.

"If not, I would have lost precious seconds," she knew, "and I wouldn't have been able to win."

On her back, Kali had initially had trouble swimming straight. Her coach had taught her to look down the tip of her nose at the point from where she had started.

"Then you'll be going straight as a whistle," he had said.

"Such a simple thing," she thought, "yet so important."

"Congratulations girl," the coach complimented her, "you have done me proud."

A photographer took her picture as she was receiving her medals. The picture appeared in the sports page of the newspaper next day, with a

The Gift

caption that read, "Twelve-year-old shows great promise."

The picture was framed and hung in their sitting room. Her dad made sure that every visitor saw it! And this was the same picture her dad was looking at one night, when alone in the house. Kali and her mum had gone to visit some relatives. Suddenly the lights went out.

Kali's dad remembered that today there would be load-shedding in their area. He lit some candles and the flickering light cast weird shadows around the room.

In the flickering yellow light, he looked at Kali's photo for a long moment, and thought about his precious daughter…

CHAPTER 2
DARK AS NIGHT

When she had first arrived on earth it was exactly midnight. The heavy clouds had hidden the moon and the stars. It was pitch dark outside. In the bright lights of the hospital delivery room, the mother had looked at her child and murmured, "You are as dark as the night, but your eyes sparkle like the stars. I shall name you Kalawati."

However, as she grew up, her parents, friends and relatives found the name to be too long. Soon everybody called her simply Kali.

And this was how she came to be called Kali, meaning, a dark female, and in Hindu mythology, the Goddess of courage and valour. She grew up into young childhood under the bright sun of her hometown, Birganj. The hot sun further darkened her already dark complexion, and it seemed no name could have been more appropriate.

Dark as Night

Her dark complexion, however, could not hide her strong character and her warm heart. Kali was affectionate and friendly towards all. She was a brave little girl who would not hesitate to climb the tallest trees when challenged to do so. Her small square chin proclaimed a determined character, and her large sparkling black eyes, her adventurous spirit.

Being an active soul, Kali often had to be scolded for coming in late for lunch.

"Where's that girl?" her mother had to wonder many a time, "she's always late for her lunch."

"She'll be in soon, don't worry," her husband always had to assure her, "she must be playing with friends." He was much more understanding in such matters than his wife. She was the type to get flustered quite easily.

Kali was the captain of the junior school sports team. She liked to play each and every kind of game and was quite good in many of them. She liked to play tennis sometimes, although the racket often seemed too big for her! Her favourite, of course, was swimming.

Twice a week she went with her dad to the city's brand new swimming pool.

"Okay, Kali, that's enough for today," she often had to be admonished, "you've been in the pool for two hours already."

The Dark Mermaid

And Kali's usual response would be, "Dad, please, just a few more minutes. Please."

Her dad, seeing his only child enjoying herself so much, would, as usual, have to give in. Never mind that the few more minutes would, more often than not, extend on for much more than that, before Kali would reluctantly drag herself out of the water!

One evening, as her dad watched her swim from end to end, without much effort, it seemed to him, he had had a thought, "It's time I enlisted her in a training course. I don't think I can teach her any more."

"As it is, now she is a better swimmer than I ever could be," he had admitted to himself. "Of course, I didn't get to learn to swim until I had almost past my teens," he excused himself!

He didn't want his daughter to have the same excuse. He knew that she loved to be in the water, and the way she had learnt so much so quickly, she certainly had talent.

"My daughter's like a fish in the water," he often boasted to his friends.

The swimming instructor had been coaching a group of boys at the far end of the pool. Walking over to him, he had asked, "Coach, is it possible for my daughter to join this group?"

"How old is she?" the coach had enquired, looking over at the melee of swimmers at the other end of the pool.

"She's twelve," Kali's dad pointed out his daughter. "There she is, the girl doing the backstroke."

"Oh, her?" the coach had noticed the dark-complexioned girl many times. He had been quite impressed with her swimming. In fact, he had been in half a mind about suggesting that she could join the training course.

'I've seen her here often. She looks promising," he had replied, "Of course, she can join this training group. But she will be the only girl in the group, I must tell you."

Kali's dad had been delighted to know that the coach had such a favourable impression of his daughter.

"She's okay, I guess," he affirmed modestly, "And it shouldn't matter if she's the only girl in the group. In fact, she will have to compete harder, which I would think would be good for her."

"Of course, with your coaching she could become much better," he added.

"Sure, she will," the tall and lanky coach had responded, beaming. He liked to be flattered!

His training group consisted of a dozen boys who were from various local schools. They were all aged between ten and thirteen.

The Dark Mermaid

"Having a girl in the group should motivate them to train harder," he thought with some shrewdness. He usually had to give a good bawling off to one or the other in order to get them to concentrate on their training! Kids were after all kids, and quite playful. It was hard to make them serious about their training.

Aloud, he had said, "Well, your daughter, you said her name is Kali, right?"

Kali's father had nodded his head. "Yes, that's right, Coach."

"Well, she can start from tomorrow itself, if that's no problem to you. Or to her. But she will have to be at the pool five days a week. Every evening at five thirty sharp."

"That's fine, Coach," Kali's Dad agreed with enthusiasm, "She'll be here from tomorrow. Five thirty sharp."

Returning home in their old and rusty 1983 Nissan car, Kali had asked, "That was a long talk you had with the swimming instructor, Dad. What was it about?" Kali had seen him talking with the coach.

"You'll be joining his training course, Kali," he had replied, "From tomorrow. Hope that's all right with you."

She had exclaimed gleefully, "I can't wait to start, Dad."

Dark as Night

"It's five days a week. Evenings. Five thirty sharp, the coach has said." He had been, to say the least, pleased to see his daughter so happy.

"Now you wait and see, Dad," Kali had exclaimed, her coal black eyes sparkling, "I'll be a champion swimmer someday. I know I will."

"Well, first you have to be good enough to beat the others in your group," he had replied cautiously, "I must tell you that all of them are boys!"

Kali had paused for only a while, before responding confidently, "So what Dad, I'll beat all of them, you just wait and see."

"She really might," he had been pleased at her confidence.

For the next one month, he had accompanied his daughter five evenings a week to her training. He had watched with keen interest as the tall coach taught his daughter how to swim better and faster. He himself had begun to be quite an expert from watching the training day after day.

"Okay, all of you," the coach often had to speak sharply to get the children's attention. "Listen to me carefully."

And the very next moment he would have to bawl, "Hey you, Jigme! What's the matter with you? Line up, I said. Now no fooling around, you hear?"

Then, again, "Pravin, what are you doing? Why are you not in line? What? You have a stomach

The Dark Mermaid

ache? You'll be all right, don't worry. Get back in line now."

Kali had been by far the most obedient of the lot and soon was the coach's favourite. Since she was a girl, the boys didn't seem to mind too much! Anyway, to Kali all the boys seemed more interested in creating mischief than in training! She herself tried to follow the coach's instructions sincerely.

"Wonder why they are in training if they are not serious about it?" she had asked herself.

In time, however, Kali had realised that many of the boys were good swimmers and had been put into training by their respective schools.

"But boys will be boys, I guess," she had said to her father, sounding wise for her age.

"You may be right Kali," he had replied, "but I guess the coach can handle them. Of course, the boys should show more interest. They seem to be quite good, you know?"

"That they are, Dad," Kali replied, "but they could become better if they were to train harder."

"That they certainly can," he had said, "Anyway, as far as I am concerned, I would like to see that you improve with training. There will be practice races tomorrow, that's what the Coach said. Think you'll win, Kali?"

Dark as Night

"I should hope so, Dad," Kali had been confident, "I think only the tall thin boy will be difficult to beat. He is so tall."

"Yes, I have noticed," he had agreed, "and though you're also quite tall for your age, still he has a definite height advantage. He will surely take the lead in the beginning. As it is, your own start is not so good."

He had been referring to her inability to keep her legs straight while diving in at the start.

"I will try to catch him at the turn, Dad," she had responded, "Don't worry. I know I can beat him if I really try hard. I'll try to turn fast at the end of the first lap."

Kali had gone to bed early that night.

"Thank God for once she's gone to bed on time," her mother had said with a sigh, as she and her husband were watching television in the living room. Kali usually had to be run off to bed most nights. She wanted to watch the sports programs as late as she possibly could.

"She is a wise girl, Mina," her husband had remarked, "she knows what's good for her. We're very lucky to have such a clever daughter."

The next day Kali had won two of the five practice races. The other three had been won by the tall boy. Kali's father had been very proud of her achievements.

The Dark Mermaid

Next day in his office, he had boasted about it to his colleagues, adding, "I don't have a lot of money but I have a nice family. Some people have lots of money but don't have a good family life. Money isn't everything, you know. A loving family is more important."

Now as he gazed at Kali's picture, deep in such thoughts, he repeated to himself, "Yes, I definitely am a lucky fellow. Such a helpful wife, and such a nice daughter."

The soft candlelight seemed to cast a golden glow on his daughter's face. The electricity still hadn't returned. Load shedding to conserve electricity was becoming a routine thing nowadays. It was such a nuisance, and what could one possibly do without electricity? The week before, the lights had gone off while he had been watching the Miss World contest! It had really upset him! By the time it returned, the winner had been announced.

Today, however, he was not very upset, lost as he was in pleasant thoughts about his family, and, especially, about his beloved daughter. He looked at the picture again and thanked God, "Thank you Lord for giving me such a nice family. I know I am a very lucky man."

He spoke too soon. Fate had other ideas for him and his family.

CHAPTER 3

A CURSE

It was when she was studying one evening that fate struck a cruel blow. Kali felt a tightening in her chest and found it difficult to breathe. Her breathing became laborious and every time she exhaled, a wheezing sound escaped her lips.

Gasping, she stumbled to her father's side.

"What's the matter, Kali?" her father asked worriedly.

"Dad, I'm finding it hard to breathe," Kali gasped, "and my chest hurts."

Her father immediately took her in his strong arms and carried her over to the sofa. Putting a couple of cushions under her head, he called out to his wife, "Mina, bring a glass of water, please."

His wife came with the water and seeing a gasping Kali, inquired anxiously, "What's the matter with our daughter? What's wrong, Kali?"

The Dark Mermaid

Her husband replied soothingly that it looked like their daughter had a mild allergy attack.

"She will be all right soon," he said. However, he was a bit worried. He worked in a pharmaceutical company and he guessed that his daughter was having an asthmatic attack.

"It must have been due to some allergy," he thought to himself, "or maybe it's something she ate."

Asking his wife to keep Kali calm, he slipped out to the corner pharmacy for some medicines. He was back shortly and gave his daughter a syrupy medicine. In a little while, Kali seemed to have become better and was breathing more comfortably. After a glass of warm milk, Kali was put to bed.

"I'll take her to the doctor tomorrow," he assured his wife.

"Will she be able to sleep well?" asked his wife, her voice still anxious, "Do you think it's anything serious?"

"No, no, Mina," her husband replied, "it's just a mild case of allergy. Don't you worry, I've given her medicine. She should have no trouble sleeping." That night, however, he himself couldn't sleep for a long time. His thoughts were troubled.

"Poor Kali," he thought, "I pray she hasn't inherited asthma from her grandfather. Oh!

A Curse

Lord Almighty, let it not be so."

He tossed and turned in bed.

"If she has asthma, how will she manage," he said to himself, "she's such an active sports girl."

The next day he took her to the doctor, who after examining Kali, said, "symptoms look like seasonal asthma to me. You know, a lot of children are affected in this way during this season. Could be due to all the pollen in the air."

"Will it go away, doctor?" asked Kali in a small voice.

"Well, I cannot say right now Kali, but we will know in due time," he replied honestly. He further added, "I'll prescribe some medicines for you. You will be all right."

"What about food, doctor?" asked her father. "Should she stop eating anything?"

"Actually it's difficult to say without an allergy test," the doctor answered, "But as a general rule, she should avoid citrus foods like oranges, and I would advise her not to eat fish for the time being."

"And yes," he looked at Kali, "Don't overexert yourself, okay?"

"What about swimming, doctor?" Kali asked anxiously, "Can I swim?"

"Of course, you can, child," he assured her, "In fact, I suggest that you continue to do regular exercises. In fact swimming is a very good exercise

The Dark Mermaid

for asthmatic people as there is less likelihood of having allergens around. It's good for you. Only remember not to overexert."

"That's a relief!" exclaimed her dad, "Isn't it, Kali?"

"Super, Dad," Kali said. "as long as I can continue swimming, its fine."

"But Kali, don't overexert yourself," the doctor warned her again.

For the next few days Kali could only sit and watch enviously as her classmates raced each other in school during lunch hour. One day, not able to contain herself, she too joined them. A short moment later she had to sit down panting for breath. It took a while for her breathing to return to normal.

However, she did go swimming almost daily, but here too she found that she couldn't swim very fast or for very long without running out of breath. Swimming at a slow pace and for one or two laps gave her no trouble. But the moment she picked up the pace or swam longer distances, she experienced a wrenching sort of pain in her chest and found it difficult to breathe. She also could hear wheezing sounds in her chest.

After a week the doctor examined her again and spoke with more certainty, "Kali, you'll have to continue with your medicines for some time."

A Curse

"When will she be all right doctor," her dad asked. "When can she stop the medicines?"

The doctor thought for a moment and then replied, "I really can't say. I would think until at least the season is over. Allergy tests need to be done. We can see what she is allergic to. But chances are, if she's allergic to one thing, she could be allergic to others too."

He added, "I gather her grandfather too had asthma. In that case, she could very well have inherited the disease. However, there are plenty of good medicines nowadays."

"So, she will have to keep on having the medicines, is that what you are telling me, doctor?" her dad was not at all happy with the doctor's reply.

"Well, at least for this season," the doctor replied. "Anyway, we will also do her allergy test tomorrow."

A few days afterwards, when the results of the tests had come in, the doctor and Kali's dad had a long talk.

"Well," the doctor sighed, "It looks like Kali is allergic to a lot of things, dust and smoke being the major ones. As well as to strong scents, like perfume and chemical smells. And I don't think high humidity is good for her either."

"But doctor," Kali's dad protested, "Birganj has a lot of smoke and dust. The humidity is also pretty high as far as I know. What can I do?"

"If you want my advice," the doctor said kindly, "I would suggest that you put her in some school in a hill station. You know, where there is little pollution and the humidity is also low."

"Will she have to continue taking medicines there also?" asked Kali's dad.

'I think she will probably be much better after some time there," answered the doctor, "I know of many asthmatic children who have done as I have just suggested. They seem to be doing quite well."

"You mean she will not suffer from asthma?" Kali's father asked with new hope.

"Well, yes," said the doctor. "She's young. There is every chance that she should be free from the disease in time. You know, sometimes asthma just disappears, as the child grows older. It has happened to many children."

"Thank you very much, doctor," Kali's father rose, "but tell me, wouldn't Kali have faster relief if she were to take an inhaler?" He was referring to the small canisters containing asthma medicine that is sprayed into the mouth through a plastic tube.

"You are right," the doctor answered, "But I don't want Kali to become dependent on medicines. You know I have seen some patients become too dependent on inhalers and take them

A Curse

even when they don't need to. Mind you, inhalers are an excellent way to take medicines and are really very effective if used properly."

"You are right, doctor," said Kali's father, "I'll talk to my wife about your suggestion."

"Good," said the doctor, "let's hope your daughter becomes better. I know she will. Then there will be no need for her to take any medicines. The mountain air in the hill stations is really very rejuvenating, you know."

CHAPTER 4
A NEW BEGINNING

That night, after Kali had gone to bed, her parents had a serious discussion.

Mr. Nigam Nepali sat on his favourite sofa. He was a heavily built man of medium height, with penetrating eyes beneath bushy eyebrows. He had a wide forehead and thick black hair. He was forty-two years old.

Swirling the ice cubes in his drink, he spoke softly to his pleasant faced, homely looking wife. "Look Mina, the doctor is right. Kali cannot have a normal life here in Birganj. No doubt this is a convenient place to live in, but the heat is unbearable most of the year. The humidity is also high and how can one escape the dust and the smoke? So many trucks and buses! I cannot stand Kali living like a sick girl. Always dependent on medicines."

Mrs. Nepali, her long black hair framing her oval face, was quiet for a moment. Then abruptly,

A New Beginning

she asked, "But what can we do? Sending our daughter away will be so hard for me. Besides, where can we send her?"

"I know it will be hard without her," replied her husband, "but it's for her best. I was thinking of Darjeeling. There are some excellent schools there."

"That's so far away," lamented Mrs. Nepali, "and won't it be terribly expensive? Wouldn't it be better to send her to Kathmandu?"

"I had thought about that," Mr. Nepali spoke in a soothing voice, "but I hear the pollution there is worse than in Birganj."

"Is that so?" Mrs Nepali wondered, "I read in the papers that the government has been trying hard to control it."

"You are right," agreed Mr. Nepali, "but I think it will take some time. They have banned diesel-driven three-wheelers and they are planning to ban vehicles more than twenty years old from the valley. However, I gather it will take a lot of time. Anyway, Kathmandu is not suitable at the moment for Kali. That's for sure."

"But isn't it very difficult to get admission in Darjeeling? How will you manage it?" she wanted to know, her large eyes doubtful.

"I have taken care of that," answered her husband, "You remember my friend, Raj Pradhan?

The Dark Mermaid

You know, we stayed in his house once while in Darjeeling. Remember him?"

"Yes, of course I do," acknowledged his wife, "as well as his wife. She was very pretty, wasn't she?" She cast a sharp glance at Mr. Nepali.

"Yes, yes," her husband grunted.

He added quickly, "He teaches English in Mount Hermon School. I gave him a call from the office this morning. He wants us to come to Darjeeling immediately. He says there are still two weeks left before school reopens."

"Did you ask him whether there were any places left?" Mrs. Nepali was aware that her husband was often too optimistic for his own good. She certainly didn't want to make such a long journey only to have to return empty-handed.

Mr. Nepali was positive, "Raj says there's a good chance. With his help, I'm sure we can get Kali admitted."

His wife had another question, "What about money?"

She was all too aware that they had practically no savings. Her husband's salary was barely enough to keep the household running. And of course, the rising cost of living was making things more difficult.

"Don't worry about that," her husband assured her, "I'll manage it."

A New Beginning

Two days later, they took the night bus to the border town of Kakarvitta. It was a ten-hour drive. The bus was packed, and most of the passengers had fallen asleep by the time they had travelled a few hours. Kali's mother soon had her head on her husband's shoulder and both were snoring softly. Kali, however, could not sleep. She kept on peering at the dark forests beside the road. She also studied the passengers inside the bus. In the dim light, she saw that three men up in front had long beards and thick moustaches.

She knew that a night bus had been looted just a few days back on this very road. The papers had reported that some of the robbers had boarded the bus in Birganj as ordinary passengers. At a place where their friends were waiting, they had forced the driver, at gunpoint, to drive into the forest on one of the jungle tracks. Taking all the passengers' valuables, they had swiftly vanished into the dense woods.

"I'd better keep a sharp lookout," thought Kali, "those three men are probably robbers."

She knew that the robbers had never been caught. They were also suspected to have robbed many other buses during the past year. "Maybe I should tell Dad," the thought went through her head, "but he's sleeping so soundly."

The Dark Mermaid

She didn't want to wake him up. "First better to be sure," she said to herself, "otherwise I'll look stupid!"

The speeding bus ate away the miles. The smooth drive and the constant lulling sound of the engine soon had Kali struggling to stay awake. Her eyelids grew heavy and once or twice she had to jerk her eyes open.

But, soon, her eyes closed, her head drooped, and she was fast asleep.

The sound of many voices awoke her. Her eyes flew open. It was daylight. She looked at her watch and saw that it was five o'clock. Groggily, she looked out of the window. They were at a bus stop. A large signboard proclaimed that they were in Kakarvitta. Many people, carrying bags, were hurrying here and there.

Suddenly she remembered the three bearded men. She craned her head out of the window and saw the three walking away from the bus. They were dressed in flowing orange robes. Their hair was long and matted. They were carrying bundles wrapped in deerskin.

"Had a sound sleep, Kali?" her dad asked, helping her down from the bus. Then, seeing the look on his daughter's face, "Is something wrong, Kali?"

A New Beginning

"Actually Dad, I thought those three bearded men were robbers," Kali confessed, pointing them out to him.

Looking at whom his daughter was pointing to, he laughed.

"You mean to say you were watching them the whole night?" he exclaimed.

"Well, yes, Dad," Kali replied with a sheepish grin, "but I fell asleep later on."

"Mina, did you hear that?" he said turning towards his wife, "Our daughter stayed awake the whole night to keep us safe. Isn't she a brave little girl?"

Smiling, she cuddled Kali, and said, "That she is. But don't let your imagination run away with you, dear."

"Yes Kali, you should have asked me," her dad added, "They are sadhus, you know. Didn't you see what they were wearing? They are probably going on a pilgrimage in India."

"Well, so much for catching robbers! " Kali said to herself, quite embarrassed.

After breakfast, they made use of the restaurant's bathroom to freshen up. Then they carried their luggage to the customs office to have their bags checked. On the other side of the check post, was a row of vehicles waiting to take passengers to Darjeeling.

The Dark Mermaid

Kali chose a green jeep that looked spanking new. The driver introduced himself as Sonam. He was short statured. Stocky in build and ruddy-faced, he had a friendly air about him.

As they drove towards Siliguri, the Indian town on the other side of the border, Kali asked, "Dad, it's still so hot and muggy here. Just like in Birganj. Isn't it supposed to be cool here?"

"No, Miss," Mr. Sonam had overheard her, "until we start climbing up to Darjeeling, the weather is quite hot."

"Yes, Kali," affirmed her dad, "you'll see. Just wait till we start going up."

They reached the big and bustling city of Siliguri after about forty minutes. They didn't stop at the town. About ten miles on, the road began to wind its way uphill. Dark green forests of tall pine trees surrounded them. They seemed to be moist with dew.

Through her open window Kali felt the air getting cooler. "It smells nice, doesn't it, Dad?" she remarked.

"Must be due to the pine trees, Kali," he opined.

There were also plenty of eucalyptus trees, with smooth white trunks. Among such fine scenery, they drove on steadily up the winding road. After half an hour, Kali saw Siliguri, the town they had left behind, thousands of feet below them.

A New Beginning

Now a swirling white mist surrounded them. "It's like driving through the clouds," exclaimed Mrs. Nepali.

There were some interesting things painted on rocky hillsides along the road. One read, "It's better to be late, Mr. Driver, than to be "The Late Mr. Driver!""

Another read, "Drive slow and you will see the hills, drive fast and you will surely see hell!"

"I am sure Mr. Sonam must be reading all these," Kali hoped fervently.

She was not the sort to scare easily, but Kali was a little more than anxious now. There were hairpin bends at short intervals on the road and it seemed the driver was blowing his horn almost non-stop. There was a constant stream of buses, trucks and cars to and fro on the narrow road. One side of the road overlooked deep valleys of green forest all along the way. To add to her anxiety, the light swirling mist had now become fog.

Mrs. Nepali too was quite anxious, "One can hardly see the road now. Mr. Sonam, are you sure you can see it?"

Mr. Sonam put on his lights and replied reassuringly, "Of course, Madam. There's no need for worry."

Kali asked, "Mr. Sonam, why are your lights yellow?"

The Dark Mermaid

"Oh, that's to see through the fog, Miss. They are fog lights, you know." The yellow lights did cut through the thick fog but sometimes it was so thick that the driver had to drive at a very slow speed, getting his bearings from the railings along the side of the road.

"Shouldn't we stop, Mr. Sonam?" Kali's mum was now very anxious.

"Madam, the fog is the thickest here because we are at quite a height," he replied, "Just a few more miles, and it will get better." Just as he had said, the fog did begin to thin out a short while later and Kali and her mum or heaved a sigh of relief.

They stopped beside a small garden along the road. A small waterfall gushed forth from the rocks and settled in a clear transparent pool. They took a few gulps from the pool.

"Oh!" Kali exclaimed, "It's so cold. Like refrigerated water, Dad!"

"Yes, and it tastes nice too, "her mum agreed. She had regained some of the pallor lost during the last few miles through the fog!

They drove on faster now. They had now put on their woollens. It was quite chilly.

Midway to Darjeeling, they stopped once more at a crowded town called Kurseong. Here they had hot momos (meat dumplings) with a spicy sauce

A New Beginning

and thin but tasty soup. Refreshed with this sumptuous snack, they set off again.

"The momos were really delicious!" observed Kali's mother.

"That they were," agreed her husband.

Kali had a question for Mr. Sonam, "Mr. Sonam, we passed a train station. When will we see a train?"

"Of course we'll see one, Miss," he replied, "The toy train is quite famous. You must have heard about it."

"Yes, I have," admitted Kali.

Some miles out of the town, she saw a line of girls walking up on a path on the hillside. They were in school uniforms, blue and white striped ties, blue skirts and blazers.

"Dad, look up there," she said in an excited voice. "Which school are they from?"

"I don't know Kali," replied her dad. "There are a lot of good schools in Kurseong. Do you know that our Queen Aishwarya studied in St. Helen's here?"

A sharp turn ahead hid the girls from view. However, now, Kali's attention was on a familiar "choo-choo" sound coming from some distance ahead.

"The toy train!" exclaimed Kali, as the next turn brought into sight a small train chug-chugging

The Dark Mermaid

along. Grey smoke hissed out of the chimney as the tiny engine courageously pulled the small blue cabins along. As they watched, a boy jumped out of one of the cabins and, picking something up from the ground alongside the rails, ran a few steps, before jumping in!

"What's the speed of this train?" Kali asked, amused.

"Well, it takes seven hours to go from Darjeeling to Siliguri, that much I know," Mr. Sonam replied. "By car, as you know, it will take us about three hours."

"Thank God, then, that we are travelling by car," remarked Mrs. Nepali.

"Actually Madam," Mr. Sonam suggested, "If you get the time you should travel by this train at least once. It's really very relaxing, and the view is simply marvellous."

"Yes, it would be a good experience," agreed Mr. Nepali. Soon they had reached a town called Ghoom, which was shrouded in fog.

"It's always like this here," informed Mr. Sonam, "Ghoom is at a higher altitude than Darjeeling."

From then on it was all downhill. Very soon Kali was treated to the splendid sight of many houses sprawled all over the hills up ahead. There were lots of houses that had red and green roofs.

A New Beginning

It was a colourful sight. The bronze roofs of monasteries shone in the sunlight.

With mounting excitement, Kali asked, "Is that Darjeeling?"

"Yes," Mr. Sonam replied, with pride in his voice, "That is the Queen of Hill Stations!"

As they sped on, Kali saw two strikingly blue circular domes on opposite sides of the hills.

"That one on the left is the dome of the Burdwan Palace, built by the Rajah of Burdwan a long time ago. The other one is the dome of the Governor's House," Mr. Sonam informed them.

A little while later they entered the town. Wooden houses, mostly small in size, lay all along the two sides of the road. Many had small verandas with potted plants on them. Most of the small windows had frilly white curtains.

"Some of them are like dolls' houses!" remarked Kali. There were also some big cement houses in places. Colourful hoardings on the roadsides advertised hotels with charming names.

Lots of people were out on the streets. All were dressed in warm clothes and many had woollen caps on. Rosy-cheeked children could be seen scampering here and there. Young boys and girls were strolling besides the road, deep in conversation.

The Dark Mermaid

"The people are so fair and rosy-cheeked here, aren't they, Dad?" observed Kali.

"That seems to be the case, Kali," her dad replied. Kali didn't notice him give her a sidelong glance.

"I should think," Kali's mum remarked unthinkingly, "You will also be fairer after some time here,"

"I hope I am," agreed Kali.

She didn't notice Mr. Sonam cast a doubtful look towards her.

CHAPTER 5
THE PRADHANS

They took a sharp turn and drove up a side street. It was a steep climb. Passing a big school building with the name 'Turnbull High School' written over huge wooden doors, the jeep went around another bend, still climbing steeply. At the top of the climb, the road levelled out on to a tree-lined street. There were beautiful houses on both sides of the road. This was obviously a posh locality.

Kali saw a castle-like stone building on the hillside, some distance above the street. It had turret-like structures and a wide stone path led up to it.

"That's the Oberoi Hotel," pointed out Mr. Sonam, "Many film stars stay there while in Darjeeling."

"Do many film stars come to Darjeeling?" asked Kali excitedly.

"Oh yes, throughout the year except during the monsoons," replied their driver. "A lot of films are shot in this town."

"We might get to see a film shooting, Dad," said Kali hopefully.

"I have watched one Kali," her dad informed her, "but it's very boring. They shoot the same scene again and again and again. It's a waste of time, that's all it is."

"I think I would find it interesting," Kali said. She knew she would love to watch her favourite film stars in action.

As they passed the Oberoi Hotel, Mr. Nepali instructed the driver to slow down so that he could read the road signs better.

"My friend's house is a little ahead. We have to take a lane going left," he said to Mr. Sonam. "The house is called 'Pradhan's Cottage'."

A little ahead, the car swerved on to a lane going left. They all peered at the names of the houses they passed. Most of them were very pretty cottages with little gardens in front.

"There it is!" exclaimed Kali, "That red cottage. See, 'Pradhan's Cottage' is written on the gate."

"Yes, so it is," confirmed the driver, stopping the jeep in front of the wooden gates.

Kali was the first to get out. She looked at the house. It was a red-coloured, two storeyed brick house with a slanting wooden roof that was also painted red.

The Pradhans

As the driver helped her dad unload their luggage, Kali pushed open the wooden gates and stepped into a lovely garden full of pretty flowers of many different colours. Thick shrubbery surrounded the house and the garden on all sides.

A pebbled path led up to the front door. Large French windows opened on to the lovely garden. Just as her mother was saying, "Kali, be careful. There might be a dog inside!" Kali heard the excited yelping of a dog. The dog scampered towards her up the path.

"Puppy, puppy," Kali called in a friendly voice. She wasn't much afraid of dogs, and certainly not one as small as this one!

It must be an 'Apso', she guessed correctly. She knew that this friendly Tibetan breed was to be found in large numbers in Darjeeling. It was about a foot in height and a foot and a half in length. The white fur on its back was thick and plentiful. Its large black eyes were almost hidden by the long thick fur on its head.

"Come, Puppy," Kali called again, extending her hand. The dog came near and started to smell her hand cautiously. After a moment, it began to lick Kali's hand. Kali was delighted! She patted the dog and put her hand close to the dog's wet nose.

"So that you remember me later," she said to the dog.

The Dark Mermaid

"She does have a way with dogs!" remarked her dad affectionately, coming through the gate carrying a suitcase in his left hand, "Just like me, I guess!"

'Come, Puppy, come," he also called to the dog, extending his free hand.

The dog left Kali and came up to him. He gave it a couple of pats and tickled its ears. The dog seemed to like that and whimpered gratefully.

"Welcome to Darjeeling!" a hearty voice called. Kali saw a tall man, of medium build, come loping up the path towards them. He was dressed in a blue pullover and brown corduroys.

"Thanks, Raj," Kali's father shook his hand warmly, "How are you?"

"Fit as a fiddle, Nigam," Mr. Raj Pradhan replied, taking the suitcase from his hands, "Welcome, Mrs. Nepali, I hope the journey wasn't too tiring?"

"Thank you, Mr. Pradhan," Kali's mother replied, looking up at the tall man with the close cropped hair and the dashing little moustache, "Actually it wasn't so tiring, even though it was such a long journey."

"This is your daughter?" Mr. Pradhan asked, putting his hand around Kali's shoulder.

"Yes," answered Mr. Nepali, "See, she's made a friend of your dog already!"

The Pradhans

"Uncle, what's its name?" Kali asked, petting the dog.

"Her name is Julie," he answered, "She seems to like you."

"She likes my dad too, right Dad?" said Kali.

"Well, Raj, you see, both of us love dogs," said Mr. Nepali, "and the dogs also seem to like us."

"We must have been dogs in our previous lives!" he added.

"Right, Dad," agreed his daughter, "Dogs are much better-looking than humans, aren't they Uncle?" she asked Mr. Pradhan.

"Absolutely, child, absolutely. I couldn't agree more!" Mr. Pradhan agreed, with an amused chuckle. Kali thought that the polka-dotted scarf around his throat made him look positively gallant. Kali liked him immediately.

They paid Mr. Sonam, who bid goodbye after giving them his visiting card with a telephone number.

"Please do call me anytime you need a taxi, Sir," he said to Kali's dad.

Mr. Raj Pradhan ushered them inside the carved wooden doors that led straight into a sitting room. Kali looked around the room with interest. It was a tastefully decorated room. The comfortable-looking sofas were made of bamboo. The large white cushions had yellow flowers painted on

The Dark Mermaid

them. At one corner of the room was a big glass-fronted cupboard displaying dozens of lovely dolls, as well as lots of silver curios. In another corner, a rosewood cabinet had a television on it. There was an antique-looking record player on its lower shelf.

There was a round table made of carved wood in front of a large French window. Its legs were curved and also carved. A wide-mouthed copper vase holding a dozen long-stemmed white flowers stood on it. The floor was covered with a dark blue Tibetan carpet with pictures of golden dragons breathing orange fire.

As they were admiring the room, a beautiful middle-aged lady in a pink sari came in through another door and exclaimed, "Hello, Mr. Nigam! Hello Mina! My oh my, it's been such a long time since the last time you were here!"

"Hello, Mrs. Pradhan!" Kali's father said warmly. Kali was amused to see that he was looking a little flustered. "Yes, it's been some twelve years now, I think. Isn't that so, Mina?" he said turning towards his wife.

"Yes, Dear," she answered, looking at her husband shrewdly. Then, turning towards Mrs. Pradhan, "Hello, Pushpa. You are looking as beautiful as ever!"

The Pradhans

"Is this your daughter?" Mrs. Pradhan asked, looking at Kali, "Oh my! I didn't know she was so big!"

"Kali blushed and protested, "Auntie, I am not so big. Some of my friends are bigger than me!"

Mrs. Pradhan laughed. Kali marvelled at how white and even her teeth were. She had such a nice smile. Kali liked her also immediately.

"How was the trip, Mina?" she asked.

She had such a nice voice too, thought Kali.

"Oh, it was all right, Pushpa," she replied, "Where are the children?"

"They have gone to see a movie," answered Mrs. Pradhan, looking at her watch, "They should be here any moment now."

"You know Ashish, of course," said Mr. Pradhan, "I don't think you have seen Reva."

"Yes, Ashish was, I think, four years old when we were here last," said Mr. Nepali, "He must be fourteen now, thats correct, Raj?"

"Yes, and Reva, our daughter, is twelve," said Mr. Pradhan.

"Where do they study, Uncle?" asked Kali, "And in which class?"

"Well, Ashish is in St. Paul's in the eleventh standard. Reva is in Mount Hermon. She's in class eight," answered Mr. Pradhan.

The Dark Mermaid

As they were making small talk, a maidservant brought in warm cookies and hot tea in large pink mugs. Kali sipped her tea slowly. It was piping hot. It had such a nice aroma.

"Auntie," she said turning towards Mrs. Pradhan, "the tea tastes so nice."

"It should be," remarked Mrs Pradhan. "After all, it *is* Darjeeling tea, you know."

"Yes dear," Kali's mum added, "Darjeeling is famous all over the world for its tea."

"It tastes different from Nepali tea," Kali observed with a wise air.

"I'm glad you like it," remarked Mr. Pradhan. "But you know, even the best Darjeeling tea can be ruined if not prepared correctly."

"Why, I also know how to make tea, Uncle," piped Kali. "All you have to do is boil milk and put sugar and tea into it. Right, Mum?"

Laughing heartily, Mrs Pradhan asked, "Kali dear, is that how you make your tea in Nepal?"

"Yes Auntie," replied Kali, "It's so easy!"

"Actually dear, that is not the way we prepare tea here," said Mrs. Pradhan in a kind tone. "We first boil the water and afterwards we pour it through a strainer containing the tea leaves. Only then do we add a little milk and sugar. In fact, we use very little milk."

The Pradhans

"Oh, you have tea leaves! That must be why it's different!" Kali exclaimed. "We don't have tea leaves. We only get dust tea in Nepal. Right, Dad?"

"Well, that's not correct Kali," her father replied, "Leaf tea is available in Nepal, but it's frightfully expensive!"

"Here too it's not so inexpensive really," interjected Mr. Pradhan. "It depends on the quality. But, of course, it must be much more expensive in Nepal."

"Anyway Kali, why are you worried?" asked her dad. "You will now be able to have all the Darjeeling tea you like."

Just then Julie, the Apso dog, began yelping shrilly. She sounded as if she was delighted.

"Down, Julie, down!" Kali heard a young girl shout.

"Sit, Julie, sit!" a young boy's voice commanded.

Suddenly, there was a whoosh of air from the open doors and two youngsters came bounding in.

CHAPTER 6

STUBBORN HORSE

The two youngsters stopped short on seeing guests in their living room. The boy was tall and well built. The girl was a foot shorter. She had short black hair and well-set features. Both had colour on their cheeks and looked robustly healthy.

"This is Ashish. Ashish, do you remember Nigam Uncle and Mina Auntie? They stayed here once," Mrs. Pradhan said, "And this is Reva."

The handsome teenager shook his head and mumbled shyly that he didn't remember. Reva smiled brightly at everyone. Her smile was as nice as her mother's.

"This is Kali," their mother said, introducing her. "She will be joining your school, Reva."

"Will you be in my class, Kali?" asked Reva.

As Kali was thinking of what to say, Mr. Pradhan interjected, "Yes, dear, Kali might well be in the same class as you."

"That's great!" exclaimed Reva, "Then we can go to school together."

"Well, not exactly," corrected Mr. Nepali, "You see, she will be staying in the hostel. Of course, you might be together in the same class."

"Why don't you take a little rest and maybe freshen up?" suggested Mrs. Pradhan, "Then we can talk more during lunch."

They were shown to their rooms on the upper floor. Kali shared Reva's room, while her parents had the room next door. Kali was momentarily fascinated with posters of many pop groups all over the walls. Reva, it seemed, certainly liked music! A cassette player stood on an untidy table full of knickknacks. Magazines were scattered all over the floor.

"Sorry about the mess," apologised Reva, sounding not the least bit sorry, "I didn't get time to clean the room."

"No, its fine," assured Kali, "In Birganj, my room is also always in a mess!"

It was true she couldn't keep her room as tidy as her mother would have liked, but it definitely wasn't as untidy as Reva's!

They had a late, late, lunch and ate at a leisurely pace.

Outside, the clouds were quite heavy and dark. Although the lunch was a simple affair of rice,

The Dark Mermaid

lentil soup and chicken curry accompanied by a spicy pickle, they enjoyed it very much.

They were, to say the least, very hungry indeed!

"I had thought Kali would be staying with us," spoke up Mrs. Pradhan, "We would love to have her with us, isn't that right, Raj?"

"Yes, Nigam," Mr. Pradhan added, "Kali can stay here. It would be no problem at all."

Mrs Nepali gave a knowing glance at her husband. She knew very well that he would never agree to have his daughter stay with the Pradhans.

"You know Mina," he had once confided to her, "When I was a kid, my father sent me to Kathmandu for my studies. I stayed with my uncle and aunt. They had two children of their own and I wasn't too comfortable living there. Although they were all very nice to me, I always had the feeling that I was imposing on them."

"But why?" Kali's mother had asked, "After all, they were your close relatives."

"Well, you see, Mina," he had searched for the right thing to say, "Even as a child I was a pretty sensitive fellow. And many a night I slept hungry because I refused second helpings, pretending I was full. I used to be very shy!"

"You shouldn't have done that!" his wife had exclaimed, "You were a growing child, you needed to eat well."

"You are right, of course," he had replied, "Maybe, today I would have been taller by an inch, who knows? But anyway, I just didn't feel comfortable."

Mrs. Nepali smiled to herself, thinking how naïve her husband must have been in his younger days.

She was brought out of her reverie by Mrs. Pradhan's words, "Why, Mina, what are you thinking of? You seem to be lost in pleasant thoughts."

"No, no," Kali's mother protested, "It's just that I was thinking about something Nigam said to me once."

"I hope it's about something good," remarked her husband, looking at her affectionately.

Kali was happy to see her parents so affectionate towards each other. In the past, she had been witness to a lot of quarrels at home. Sometimes she would be scared that the quarrels might lead them to divorcing each other.

Both her parents were quite outspoken when angry. Even her homely-looking mother; whom she had always thought to be mild in nature.

However, there had been very few quarrels in the last few years.

"Hope it stays like that," Kali thought to herself.

The Dark Mermaid

"What about Kali's admission, Raj?" Mr. Nepali asked his friend.

"I have talked to the Principal. Seems there's one place left in Reva's class. A girl from Sikkim has decided not to come back this year," Mr. Pradhan replied.

"Oh, that must be Alina! In our class, she's the only one from Sikkim," exclaimed Reva, "Why isn't she coming back, Dad?"

"I gather her father has been transferred to Delhi," Mr. Pradhan answered. "She'll probably study there now."

"That's a fortunate thing to happen for us!" exclaimed Mr. Nepali.

"Kali, you certainly are a lucky girl," her mother added.

"Tomorrow is a holiday," Mr. Pradhan informed them. "We'll go to the school the day after, that is, on Monday, and get her admitted."

"That's fine," agreed Mr. Nepali, "We can also see about the hostel then. Raj, will there be a problem with that? What do you think?"

"Putting her in the hostel should be no problem at all," responded Mr. Pradhan. "However, I don't know why you can't let her stay with us."

"Really, that's very nice of you and Pushpa," Mr. Nepali was quite adamant, "but I think living in a hostel will be better for Kali."

"Yes, she can have more swimming practice," added Mrs. Nepali, diplomatically, trying to smoothen the situation.

"Oh, you like swimming, do you?" asked Mr. Pradhan.

"Yes Uncle," replied Kali, "I love to swim."

"Then, you are joining the right school," Mr. Pradhan rejoined, "Mount Hermon has an excellent swimming pool. It also has a good record in swimming competitions."

"That's great! Isn't it, Dad?" exclaimed Kali, "I hope I'll be able to take part in competitions."

"So that means you must be a good swimmer," Reva observed, "I myself don't know how to swim."

"I'll teach you, don't worry," Kali assured her, "although I'm not really such a good swimmer as you say."

With a little smile, Kali's father corrected his daughter, "Yes Reva, Kali can teach you. She's pretty good, you know."

He glanced at his wife, meeting her eyes.

Both of them had the same thought, "I didn't know Kali was such a modest girl!"

"Let me warn you, Kali," Ashish joined in the conversation at last. He was certainly the quiet type! "Teaching Reva to swim won't be easy. She's dead scared of drowning!"

The Dark Mermaid

"Come on," Reva protested loudly, "I am not! Well at least I won't be, if somebody is there to save me!"

"Well, then you needn't worry," Ashish responded, "Kali will be there to look after you. Let's hope you get to learn to swim at last!"

Now feeling a bit embarrassed with all the attention, Kali asked Mr. Pradhan, "Uncle, can we go horse riding?"

"Why don't we go tomorrow? You must be tired after such a long journey," Mr. Pradhan suggested.

"That's right," agreed Kali's dad quickly.

He didn't think he was up to horse riding today. Not after such a long drive! "Let's relax at home today. We need to rest."

After a light dinner that night, Kali and her parents went to sleep immediately. They were too tired to stay awake and watch television. In Birganj, they had always watched television quite late into the night.

Tonight Kali slept peacefully, curled up warmly under a heavy quilt. Her parents too had 'one of the best sleeps they had ever had', as Kali's father remarked the next day. They slept so like the proverbial logs, that they were completely unaware of heavy rainfall throughout the night.

They awoke feeling refreshed as only a good night's sleep can do. Kali opened the windows next

Stubborn Horse

to her bed and breathed deeply of the invigorating mountain air.

"Had a good night's sleep, Kali?" asked her mother.

"Oh yes, Mum," answered Kali.

"You know dear," remarked her dad, "You didn't take your medicine yesterday, yet you didn't have any trouble sleeping. Isn't that marvellous?"

"Let's hope she gets cured of asthma," Mrs. Nepali prayed.

"I'm sure she will," assured her husband confidently.

As they had breakfast in the dining room on the upper floor, they admired the magnificent scene from the large window. The sky had cleared after the heavy rains in the night. The sun was shining brightly, but the morning was cool and clear.

It promised to be a beautiful day. On the horizon, beyond valley after valley of green forests, the third tallest mountain in the world, Kangchenjunga, shimmered silver in the rays of the bright sun.

"What a magnificent view!" exclaimed Mrs. Nepali.

"That's for sure," agreed her husband with enthusiasm, "Raj, you are really lucky to live in such a beautiful place!"

The Dark Mermaid

Kali was also quite enamoured by the lovely spectacle, but she couldn't wait to go horse riding.

She asked Mr. Pradhan impatiently, "Uncle, when can we go horse riding?"

"Right after we finish breakfast, Kali," he replied, "Ashish, Reva, you'd better hurry up with your breakfasts. Kali is in a hurry."

It took them fifteen minutes on foot to reach Chowrasta, where the stables were. They went to the stables, where Kali chose a big white mare.

"Her name is Heena," the young groom told Kali, "She is a good horse, but sometimes she can be a little stubborn, you know?"

"That's all right, I can handle her," Kali spoke with false confidence. She had actually ridden a horse only a couple of times before. That had been a year ago, when they had gone to Pokhara, the lovely lake city in western Nepal, about two hundred kilometres from Birganj.

Reva's pony was smaller and called Panna. It was black in colour and seemed to be somewhat fidgety, or so Kali thought. It was prancing about on its toes even when standing in one place.

Ashish and Mr. Nigam rode on a black and a brown pony respectively. Mrs. Nepali and Mrs. Pradhan preferred to soak up the sun sitting on one of the green benches around the place. Mr. Pradhan gave them company.

Stubborn Horse

The riders started off at a brisk trot around the four-mile long circular mall. It started and ended in Chowrasta. Kali had a tough time holding on to the saddle horn. Reva and Ashish were quite proficient and were galloping away after a short while. Kali's dad rode along with his daughter for some time.

He had thought about hiring a groom, known as a 'Sayesh', to ride along with them, but Ashish had said, "There's really no need, Uncle. It's only a short ride."

He could see that Kali was not riding very comfortably and gave instructions as he rode along beside her.

"Keep your back straight, Kali," he said to her, "Don't slouch. It will upset your balance." And, "Grip with your knees, not with your feet."

After about a mile, he went ahead at a gallop while Kali trotted behind. Reva and Ashish were waiting for them near a couple of benches facing the mountains. From here, as from almost everywhere, they could see the beautiful Kangchenjunga Mountain.

After admiring the scenery for a few moments, they again set off. Kali promised herself that soon she would also be as good as Ashish and Reva in horse riding.

"Come on Uncle, let's race!" shouted Ashish.

The Dark Mermaid

Mr. Nepali couldn't resist the challenge and galloped after the youngster. Reva went after them at a more leisurely trot. Soon, all three of them had vanished around the curve ahead.

Kali urged her horse to go a little faster. Suddenly, her horse decided she was hungry and trotted to the side of the road to nibble at the luscious green grass. Kali tried to pull up the large head by pulling on the reins. After a while she gave up. Heena wasn't responding at all, and once even turned her head to nibble at her foot! After that, Kali just waited for her to finish her meal.

Having decided that she had eaten enough, Heena again trotted on. Around the curve, Kali saw a long stretch of road ahead, before another bend came into view. Ashish and her father had already raced around the far bend.

Reva was riding at a brisk trot, her small body jumping up and down rhythmically with the movement of the horse.

Kali called out, "Reva! Reva!" but she didn't hear and kept trotting on.

A few minutes later Kali saw Reva kick her horse and it started to gallop. Just then, Heena slowed down to a walk.

"Oh no!" Kali spoke aloud, "Not again!"

Heena had turned her head to look at bunches of wet green grass on the side of the road. Now, completely disregarding Kali's pull on the reins, she walked majestically for another delicious meal!

Kali didn't know what to do. She definitely didn't want her foot to be nibbled by a horse!

Heena gave her rider a sidelong glance from her large eyes. She seemed to be saying, "I hope I have taught you a good lesson!"

As Kali sat on the wide back of her horse, not knowing what to do, she heard the excited barking of a dog. She looked up the road.

A large black mastiff dog was running and barking at Reva's horse. Reva tried to shoo it away, but it was now running very close to her horse's legs. Kali saw Reva trying to make her horse go faster. The horse, however, was trying to turn its head to look at the barking dog. It was also making efforts to twist its body to face the dog.

Looking on, Kali became very worried. She tried to pull up her horse's head, but the stubborn beast wouldn't budge an inch. Helplessly, she looked at Reva as she tried desperately to control her nervous horse.

The horse was trying to run and twist its body at the same time. The large black dog was enjoying itself, frightening the bigger animal. It became bolder and bolder and was now snapping at the horse's heels. The horse was now tottering in its run. Reva was holding on to the saddle horn for all she was worth. Things didn't look good.

Kali pulled at the reins with all her strength. She had to go and help Reva. Ashish and her father were nowhere to be seen. Reva needed her!

But Heena, the big brute, was really more stubborn than the groom had warned her.

"Is she trying to eat all the grass on the roadside?" she thought in exasperation. She was feeling scared for Reva. She might fall. The dog might bite her. She had to go and help.

At last, the stubborn beast of a horse pulled up its head, and looking at Kali scornfully, started to canter ahead.

Kali kicked with her heels repeatedly. But the horse didn't seem to know that it was meant to speed her up. She cantered on at a slow pace. Ahead, Kali saw that the bend was coming nearer and Reva was near to it. The dog seemed to be tiring from running and barking at the same time. It had slowed down.

"Oh, now she's safe," thought Kali in relief.

The very next moment, the dog decided to scare the black horse one more time and charged at its hind legs, snapping its jaws. The horse raised its hind legs. The dog barked louder, and suddenly the horse skidded to a halt and reared up on its legs, neighing shrilly.

Stubborn Horse

Kali looked on in horror as Reva's hands flew away from the saddle horn; her body was thrown violently in the air, and then she soared high and over the fence beside the road.

CHAPTER 7

SPITTING LLAMA AND HITLER'S TELESCOPE

Kali jumped down from her horse and ran over to the side to look down the hillside. Reva lay in a heap on a narrow dusty path at the bottom of the slope.

Thankfully, the slope was a short one. Reva surely couldn't have been hurt too badly. Kali scampered over the wooden railing and slid down the grassy slope.

"Come on, Reva, get up," she pleaded, "Are you hurt anywhere?"

With a small moan, Reva sat up. "It hurts here, Kali," she said, holding the back of her head.

"Let me see," Kali said. With soft hands she explored the back of Reva's head, "Oh yes, there's a teeny weeny lump. Don't worry, it's only a small one."

Spitting Llama and Hitler's Telescope

She helped Reva to her feet. They climbed the short hillock up to the road and Kali helped her over the fence.

Reva's horse was nowhere to be seen. "It must have run back to the stable," Reva groaned, "Where's that awful dog?"

"Here it is," Kali was patting the large black mastiff on its head. The dog was wagging its tail furiously and seemed to be thoroughly proud of what it had done.

"It must be thinking it has done something great!" Reva remarked angrily.

"Oh, it's not really its fault, Reva," Kali defended the dog, "It must have thought it was playing a game." She loved dogs and didn't want to blame them for anything!

"Well, at least your horse hasn't run away," Reva observed. The white horse was busy munching the grass on the roadside, "We'll both ride it."

Kali shooed the black dog away. Then both the girls climbed up on to the broad back of the white mare. Reva kicked the horse's sides with her heels and, giving the reins a sharp jerk, commanded, "Giddap!"

The white mare didn't move at all. She was as still as a statue.

The Dark Mermaid

"What's the matter, you stubborn old horse?" Kali muttered. "Giddap, Giddap!" She too dug in her heels.

Still the horse refused to move. After a couple more tries, the girls had to give in to the brute's stubbornness. Both of them dismounted.

"We'll have to pull it along," said Reva, taking a tight grip of the reins. Kali walked beside the horse while Reva pulled it along. The large black dog followed behind. As they neared Chowrasta, the stubborn horse turned its head towards Kali. Its lips were curled over its large yellow teeth.

"I swear the big brute is grinning," Kali exclaimed! "She's letting me know that she has won!"

As they entered Chowrasta, Mr. Pradhan was the first to spot them coming, "What happened to you two? Where's your horse, Reva?"

Kali's parents and Mrs Pradhan also came over to the small group.

"Kali, you didn't fall, did you?" Mr. Nepali inquired anxiously.

"Well, actually it's I who fell down," Reva admitted, blushing a deep pink. She seemed to be embarrassed. She pointed towards the black dog, "It's all his fault!"

After she had told the anxious parents the full story, Mrs. Pradhan felt the lump at the back of Reva's head.

"I think it's only a small lump, thank God!" she said gratefully.

They found Reva's horse back in the stable. It was busily slurping water from the trough.

Kali's white mare ambled over to its side, but before dipping its head towards the water trough, it hesitated a little. Then, lifting its huge head, it looked backwards towards Kali and gave a small whinny neigh.

"I showed you, didn't I?" it seemed to be conveying, at least to Kali.

Shaking her head ruefully, Kali went over to join the others at the coffee stall.

As they drank hot coffee from paper mugs, Ashish said, "Dad, why don't we go to visit the zoo now? It will be fun!"

"Oh, let's," piped in Reva.

"You've been to our zoo before, haven't you, Nigam?" Mr. Pradhan asked Kali's father.

"No, Raj," Mr. Nepali replied, "Last time we were here, it was raining cats and dogs. Couldn't go anywhere at all."

"Well then, let's go," Mrs. Pradhan exclaimed, "It should be interesting for our visitors."

"Yes, it should be quite interesting," agreed Kali's father.

So they went off talking, laughing and enjoying the scenery of Darjeeling. The cool air was refreshing. On reaching the zoo twenty minutes later, Kali could see that it was a different sort of zoo from the ones in Kathmandu and in Calcutta, which she had seen.

There, the zoos had been more or less scattered over a vast field, with cages lined alongside stony paths. Only the tigers and the rhinos had been allowed to frolic over large vegetation-filled grounds behind tall bars.

Here the zoo was named Kamala Nehru Zoological Park. Near the entry gates, Kali saw four black bears sunbathing on a bare hillock. Around it was a wide moat full of water, and this was in turn surrounded by a shoulder-level rock wall. There were a couple of tall trees that seemed totally bare of leaves.

"The trees look so naked, Uncle," Kali remarked to Mr. Pradhan.

"Oh, its because the bears have eaten all the leaves," replied Mr. Pradhan.

"Even at the top, Uncle?" Kali asked.

"Oh yes, they are very good climbers, you know Kali," he informed her.

A little way ahead Kali noticed a small crowd on the opposite side of the road. People were peering through the strong-looking wire nets that lined the road. Different animals lived behind the nets on the wide expanse of tree-filled hillocks.

Wire netting also enclosed the other sides of the hillocks.

As Kali went over to see what people were looking at behind the nets, two Buddhist monks, known locally as lamas, took several hurried steps back. The children in the small crowd hooted with laughter.

Kali heard one of the children shout gleefully, "The Llama has spit at the Lama!"

Behind the wire nets, Kali saw a long-necked, camel-like animal, dark grey in colour. It was strutting around on long bony legs. It was a llama, the creature her father had once mentioned as being unusual, and it had spat a big glob of thick sputum at the crowd.

By sheer coincidence, the glob of sputum had landed on one of the robed lamas' face! "What a funny thing to happen!" thought Kali, laughing out aloud, "No wonder they call it 'Spitting Llama'!"

The aggrieved lama wiped his face angrily with his sleeve while his fellow monk giggled in mirth, tears in his eyes!

The llama, on hearing the hoots of laughter, strutted all the more fancifully on its long legs. Its long face, with large limpid eyes and wide mouth, seemed to convey an expression of amazed delight!

The Dark Mermaid

They left the hilarious scene and walked up the road. A short way ahead, they saw a wild buffalo and a couple of yaks grazing on the grassy slopes. Next they made their way up a long flight of rocky steps.

As Kali climbed slowly, she peered through the strong wire nets lining both sides of the steps. She could see two tigers lying peacefully together, partly hidden by shrubs. Some children up ahead were yelling at the magnificent animals and making all sorts of funny noises. They, obviously, wanted the tigers to respond by roaring. In fact, one of the larger boys was trying to imitate a roar, but Kali thought he sounded more like a kitten.

"Those are Royal Bengal Tigers," Mr. Pradhan informed them. "On the other side, are two white Siberian Tigers. If we are lucky we will also see them, although they mostly hide among the trees."

"Where are the lions?" asked Kali.

"Well, unfortunately, there are no lions in this zoo, Kali," replied Mr. Pradhan.

Suddenly, one of the tigers sprang up to its feet and let out a spine-tingling roar. The group of children jumped back as one, and in their haste, a small girl fell down backwards on the steps.

The small girl rolled down four or five steps before falling at Kali's feet. She immediately bent

Spitting Llama and Hitler's Telescope

down to help the little girl up, and saw that she was bleeding from the nose.

"Dad, please give me your handkerchief," said Kali.

She put the large white hankie to the girl's nose and told her to tilt back her head.

The little girl started to cry. Kali comforted her with, "Sshhh, don't cry. You'll be all right."

The other children had gathered around them. Two of the bigger boys who had been making most of the noise, looked sheepish. After a while, the small girl stopped bleeding and the group of children went down the steps.

"That was very nice of you, Kali," observed Mrs. Pradhan, "You are quite a capable girl."

"Yes, that's right," agreed her husband.

Kali's father proudly informed them that his daughter had received some first aid training during swimming lessons.

"That's very comforting to know," said Mrs. Pradhan.

They walked up and reached a flat plateau with a very large rock. It was surrounded by lots of trees. They had climbed almost a hundred steps. Up here, there was considerable mist. Beyond the plateau, one could see lots of hills and mountains.

A young couple was sitting with their backs against the rock. The boy had a boyish freckled

The Dark Mermaid

face, while the girl had short hair and a cute face. They seemed oblivious of everybody but themselves. They looked part of a postcard scene, what with the big black rock, the tall trees surrounding them, and the swirling mist.

Reva nudged Kali and pointed her chin at the couple, smirking mischievously. Kali smiled back, she had seen such scenes plenty of times on T.V.

"It is such a pretty scene," thought Kali.

"Shall we rest awhile?" inquired Mrs. Nepali. She was more than a little tired now.

"There's a restaurant a little ahead," said Mrs. Pradhan, "Why don't we stop there and have something to drink?"

"That's a good idea," agreed Mr. Nepali, adding, "Come on Mina, you get tired too fast. The exercise is good for you."

His wife gave him a long look. Kali thought that she must have been annoyed with her father for agreeing too often with the pretty Mrs. Pradhan.

The walk had put colour on their cheeks, even Kali's dark cheeks looked a bit darker. Mrs. Pradhan was looking more beautiful than ever, and Kali wished she could be as beautiful.

Ashish spoke up, "Dad, we must see the Mountaineering Museum."

"Of course, we will see it," agreed Mr. Pradhan.

"How far is it?" asked Mrs. Nepali anxiously.

Spitting Llama and Hitler's Telescope

'Don't worry, it's just next to the restaurant, hardly five minutes away," assured Mr. Pradhan.

"Yes, dear, only five minutes," mimicked Mr. Nepali.

Walking through the grassy path, they came upon the restaurant around the corner. It was a very small red wooden house with white plastic chairs and tables on the lawn. Nearby was a monument to the great Tenzing Norgay Sherpa. He was the first man to have climbed Mount Everest, the highest mountain on earth. The monument was made of solid black rock.

"Dad, wasn't Tenzing Sherpa from Nepal?" asked Kali.

"Of course he was, Kali," replied her dad, "He was born in Solu Khumbu District in the mountain region of Nepal."

"But I haven't seen any statue of his in Nepal," wondered Kali.

"You're right, Kali," agreed Mr. Nepali, "but I'm sure somebody will make one someday."

"They should, surely," added Mr. Pradhan, "after all, he has done all Nepalese proud."

They ordered coffee and cookies. It was nearly noon now. Clouds were beginning to cover the sun and the weather was cool and pleasant. The hot coffee was refreshing and the delicious cookies gave them new strength.

The Dark Mermaid

After resting awhile, they walked the short distance to the Himalayan Mountaineering Institute. It consisted of many long buildings. At the entrance, a wall of one building was sculpted with the figures of two mountaineers climbing a peak with the aid of a white rope.

Mr. Pradhan bought tickets for all of them.

Kali whispered to her dad, "Dad, why don't you pay for the tickets? Uncle Raj has already paid for the tickets to the zoo."

"It's okay Kali, never mind," assured her dad, smiling at his daughter's sense of consideration.

They entered the museum and looked around at the interesting items on display. The stuffed Himalayan birds and animals fascinated Kali.

In the centre of the hall, was a mock scenario of a mountaineering expedition camp in the Himalayas. There were lifelike dummies of two climbers in heavy mountain gear, a tent with all amenities required for the expedition and oxygen cylinders.

There were excellent models of mountaineers traversing crevices in the icy mountains as well as models of the Himalayan Range.

The upper floor abounded in Himalayan flora and fauna. The next hall had on display many trophies, citations and awards won by famous climbers.

Spitting Llama and Hitler's Telescope

There was also a long list of names of past conquerors of Everest. Kali looked in fascination at a lot of beautiful photographs of the brave men and women, as well as of famous mountain peaks.

After they had seen the museum, they went to the gift shop. Here they bought some nice souvenirs. There was a notice informing visitors that in half an hour's time, there would be a film show about an Everest expedition.

Kali looked at her watch. It was almost one thirty, and she was quite hungry. Everybody agreed that they would prefer to return home for a well-deserved lunch, so they did not wait to see the film.

Ashish, however, insisted that they should look through the big telescope near the hostel before going back.

"You know, I lived in that hostel while doing my Basic Adventure Course last year," he informed Kali.

"How long was the course?" asked Mr. Nepali.

"Oh, it was about a month long," replied Ashish.

"You must tell us about it sometime, Ashish," said Mr. Nepali, "I'm sure Kali would be interested."

"Sure, Uncle," replied Ashish.

As they were talking, Kali had already gone ahead to see the telescope. "Dad, it's a pretty big

The Dark Mermaid

telescope," called out Kali, "and it's written here that it was donated by Hitler! Just imagine!"

"That's really interesting to know," agreed her dad, studying the telescope. It was almost like an artillery gun, grey in colour, and with plenty of round knobs. It was huge, to say the least.

Kali put her eye to the telescope and Ashish helped her to focus it. "Dad, Mum, I can see the trees on those far off hills. They seem so near!" exclaimed Kali excitedly.

They took turns looking through the massive telescope, and Ashish informed them that sometimes one could see soldiers patrolling on those hills.

"Now, I think we should really be going back," suggested Mrs. Pradhan, "I think it's well past lunch hour now."

"Do we have to walk back?" asked Mrs. Nepali in a plaintive voice. "No, Mrs. Nepali, don't you worry, I'll manage a taxi to drive us back," assured Mr. Pradhan.

They found a taxi in the parking stand and took a different route home, passing a couple of cemeteries. Kali noticed some young couples blissfully lying down on tombstones and passing the time of day. The cemeteries were quite a pretty sight, set as they were among lots of colourful gardens.

Spitting Llama and Hitler's Telescope

After passing Government College, they saw that the hills sloping down to their right were full of small green shrubs set in neat rows. Some women could be seen plucking leaves and throwing them into cane baskets on their backs.

"That is the Happy Valley Tea Gardens," announced Mr. Pradhan. "That long building you see down below is where they produce tea from the leaves collected."

"Can we go to see the factory?" asked Kali.

"Of course, we can," answered Mr. Pradhan, "We will go to see it some other time."

En route, they crossed Chowk Bazar and Kali saw a ropeway running over the street.

"That is the ropeway which carries goods," informed Mr. Pradhan. "There's another one which carries people. We will certainly ride it later. You will enjoy it."

After lunch, while the elders retired to their rooms for some rest, Reva took Kali to a friend's house in the neighbourhood. The house was only a few blocks away. It was a big white mansion and there were a couple of cars in the driveway.

"Kali, this is my best friend, Manisha," introduced Reva. "And Manisha, this is Kali, my new friend from Nepal. She will also be studying in our school."

"Will she be in our class?" asked Manisha. She was fair, doe-eyed and very pretty. She was

The Dark Mermaid

wearing an expensive looking dress. "Yes, she will be in our class," replied Reva.

Manisha took them inside. Kali was amazed at the large number of dolls all over Manisha's room. She guessed that Manisha's parents must be very rich. In Nepal, Kali always had to wait for her birthday, or when her dad went to India, to get a doll. She liked Barbie dolls especially, but she was aware that they were quite expensive. She had just managed to collect four of them.

They played with the dolls for some time and Manisha showed Kali a large dolls' house with real-looking furniture. She seemed to have all the Barbie dolls as well as all the accessories like the house, furniture, dresses, kitchen, etc… Besides, the Barbie dolls there were a lot of other dolls, as well as many different kinds of toys. Kali was enthralled for some time.

After some time, Kali went out to the verandah to admire the garden. Reva and Manisha sat down on the big bed to talk. Manisha seemed the talkative sort and Reva was no less. As Kali went out to the verandah, their non-stop chatter followed her.

She watched some squirrels chase each other. After a while, she felt thirsty and decided to go inside. In the room, she noticed that the two friends were talking incessantly, their conversation punctuated now and then by shrill laughter.

Spitting Llama and Hitler's Telescope

They were so engrossed that they didn't notice Kali come inside and go to the corner table where there was a bottle of drinking water. Thinking that Kali was still outside, Manisha whispered loudly, "Reva, your friend is almost black!"

Reva whispered back, "Yes, that's why she's called Kali."

As she said this, she looked up and saw Kali in the room.

Blushing furiously, she blurted out, "Kali! I thought you were outside!"

75

CHAPTER 8
MOUNT HERMON

Pretending not to have overheard them, Kali said cheerfully, "I just came in to have some water. Manisha, don't you have Archie comics?" Flustered, Manisha sprang up from the bed and took out some comics from under her bed, "Here you are."

Kali said, "I think I'll read these outside on the verandah. It's so pleasant out there." As she went outside, she thought she heard Reva whisper to Manisha, "I hope she didn't hear us!" "Even if she has, we didn't say anything wrong!" retorted Manisha.

Kali's father noticed that his daughter looked a bit disturbed that evening and asked her for the reason. "It's really nothing Dad," said Kali, "I'm just a little tired that's all."

"I know you well, Kali," said her Dad, "Something's disturbing you."

Mount Hermon

"I'll tell you some other time," Kali promised.

"I'm sure you will," said Mr. Nepali.

That night they again slept very soundly. They awoke the next morning fresh as daisies.

"We sleep so well here, don't we dear?" Mr. Nepali asked his wife.

"Yes, I think we must come here more frequently for a few days of rest and recuperation," agreed his wife, "It's good for our health as well as for our peace of mind."

"With Kali studying here, we will have to come more often now," remarked Mr. Nepali.

"I wonder why more people from Nepal don't come to visit Darjeeling during holidays," wondered Mrs. Nepali. "It's not so far away and it's like a home away from home."

"You are right," concurred her husband. "They would rather go to Bombay, Delhi and such places. When, in fact, Darjeeling is so much more economical. And it's such an interesting place!"

"As they say, people neglect those that are the nearest," observed Mrs. Nepali.

They started for Mount Hermon shortly after breakfast. Walking down to Chowk Bazar, they took a taxi next to the supermarket and drove along the scenic road towards Mount Hermon, some five kilometres away. On the way, they passed St.

The Dark Mermaid

Robert's School and Loreto Convent, as well as St. Teresa's Girls' School.

Some distance ahead, they also saw Government College and St. Joseph's College. The former was a sprawling old building, while the latter looked spanking new. As they took a sharp turn downhill, they saw a castle-like stone building alongside the road, with lots of tall trees along its walls.

"That's the famous St. Joseph's School. It's also known as North Point. The King of Nepal and his brothers did their schooling here," Mr. Pradhan informed them.

"They stayed in the hostel, didn't they, Raj?" Mr. Nepali wanted to know.

"Yes, they did live in the hostel, and they were like any other average student," Mr. Pradhan said.

"Why can't I study here, Uncle?" inquired Kali.

"You can't do that dear," replied Mr. Pradhan, "It's not co-educational. It's only for boys."

"Oh I see," said Kali, "But Mount Hermon is co-educational, right, Uncle?"

"Yes that's right," said Mr. Pradhan, adding, "The well-known schools here are North Point, Mount Hermon, Loreto Convent and St. Paul's. Loreto is a girls' school, while both North Point and St. Paul's are for boys. Only Mount Hermon is co-educational."

Mr. Nepali was looking at the imposing building of North Point School with interest. "It looks like a very big school," he remarked, "and very spacious too."

"No doubt, it's a big school," agreed Mr. Pradhan, "although the number of students is less than a thousand. It also has three playing grounds."

"Why three?" Kali wanted to know, " Other schools only have one!"

"Well, there are three divisions in this school," Mr. Pradhan explained, "Primary, Lower and Upper Divisions. Each has their own playing ground."

"It must be an expensive school, then!" remarked Mrs. Nepali.

"Well, it is rich, I guess," said Mr. Pradhan. "However, it is not really that expensive for students. In fact, St. Paul's is much more expensive. And you might be interested to know, Nigam, that North Point is more than one hundred years old!"

As they were speaking, they passed the well-tended terrace garden of the school. On the opposite side, below the road, they saw a big playing ground. Mr. Pradhan pointed it out as the field for the Upper Division boys.

"This ground is also a sort of local stadium for the town. Most of the football matches are played

The Dark Mermaid

here," said Mr. Pradhan, "Many smaller schools also have their sporting events in this ground. Even the Independence Day celebrations of the town are held here each year. Yes, indeed, we have to be thankful for the generosity of the North Point School authorities!"

"That's really nice of them," said Mr. Nepali. "This school is run by the Jesuit Fathers, is it not?"

"Not only St. Joseph's but most of the better schools in Darjeeling are run by them," said Mr. Pradhan.

"And also in Kalimpong and Kurseong, right Raj?" asked Kali's dad.

"That's right, Nigam," answered Mr. Pradhan.

Shortly after crossing North Point, they reached Mount Hermon School. The first thing that struck Kali was that the school seemed to be ensconced among a lot of greenery. In fact, the whole of Darjeeling had a lot of greenery; that was what made walking such a pleasure in the town. But here the greenery seemed to be especially abundant.

There were several buildings that were quite old but well maintained. The large playground led to a big U-shaped castle-like building. It was made of grey stone and had cemented corners. There were several turrets on the top of the building.

Mount Hermon

Behind and to the side, a steel fence surrounded the tennis court. Near to it was a circular-shaped building and in front of it was the swimming pool. Behind this, one could see another big building and further away, among still more greenery, a number of small cottages.

The whole establishment was a sight for sore eyes, and Kali's heart beat a bit faster in anticipation of studying in this school. At the moment, the whole place seemed a bit empty and desolate because there were no students. School would be opening in a week's time.

They entered a large office with comfortable furniture and racks full of neatly kept files. The Principal's office was behind a door to the side and, as soon as they entered, a towering man with a white beard got up from his leather chair behind a mahogany table.

"Good morning, Mr. Pradhan," he said in a pleasant voice.

"Good morning, Mr. D'Souza," said Mr. Pradhan, "This is my friend, Mr. Nepali. And this is Mrs. Nepali and their daughter Kali. They are from Nepal."

"Lovely place, lovely place," commented Mr. D'Souza, "I was in Kathmandu last August. Please sit down."

The Dark Mermaid

He rang a bell and immediately an attendant came in. "Please get us some tea, James," the Principal ordered. "Yes, Sir," the Nepali attendant answered.

Kali thought it a little odd that he should be called James, because he looked typically Nepalese. She kept it in her mind to ask Mr. Pradhan later.

"So, you are the little girl who is joining our school!" remarked Mr. D'Souza. "You look like a smart girl."

"Thank you, Sir," replied Kali.

They had tea and Mr. D'Souza told them that school would be opening a week hence. He gave them a list of the standard things she was expected to bring with her. The list consisted of bed and bedding, clothes, shoes, and other items like toiletries etc...

"Whatever she needs is listed in that," said Mr. D'Souza. "You can pay the fees including the deposit at the cashier's desk in the next room."

Mr. Pradhan introduced them to the cashier in the next room. He was an oldish-looking fellow with a bent back. His name was Thomas. Again, Kali was surprised. He also looked like a typical Nepali. After getting the receipt for their payments, they went outside.

"Why don't I show you around the school grounds, Mrs. Nepali?" offered Mr. Pradhan.

He informed them that the U-shaped castle like structure was called the Main Building.

It had classrooms on the ground floor and a chapel on the first floor. Besides the chapel, the first floor had dormitories for boys of class one, two and three, whereas the second and third floor, as well as the attic, had dormitories for girls. The big building also had an underground dining hall.

"This is the Stewart Building," informed Mr. Raj Pradhan, pointing out a large yellow building, "It has dormitories for boys of class four and five. It also contains classrooms for classes seven to eleven. The rest of the classrooms are in the Main Building."

Adjoining the blue swimming pool, was a circular-shaped building. "That's called Round Building," Mr. Pradhan said, "All three floors have dormitories for boys of classes six, seven and eight. The warden lives in the basement."

There was another building, which, Mr. Pradhan said, was named Fern Hill. He added, "Fern Hill has dormitories for class nine and ten boys. In addition, Fern Hill houses class twelve boys in the Glass House, and class eleven boys live in the Kangchenjunga Room."

The Dark Mermaid

"Where does the staff stay?" Mr. Nepali asked.

"Oh, many of the teachers live in those cottages you see behind the Round House," answered Mr. Pradhan.

"I must say there's plenty of space around here!" remarked Mrs. Nepali. Her husband echoed the same thought.

Mr. Pradhan was pleased to see that his visitors were suitably impressed with his school.

"Well, Kali," he asked jovially, "Do you think you will like living here?"

"I think I will, Uncle," she replied.

As they drove back, Kali asked, "Uncle, why is that attendant's name James? And the cashier's, Thomas? Aren't they Nepalese?"

Smiling, Mr. Pradhan replied, "Yes, they are Nepalese, Kali. Their names are like that because they have become Christians. You will find many Nepalese with such names in Darjeeling."

"So, there are a lot of Christians in this town?" asked Mrs. Nepali.

"Oh yes, and many of them get good jobs in missionary schools. Even their children can get admission easily, and many don't have to pay any fees," replied Mr. Pradhan.

"Then, it's nice to be a Christian, right, Mum?" remarked Kali.

"Well that is their choice, there's certainly no harm in it!" said Mrs. Pradhan.

"Quite beneficial too, I must say!" put in Mr. Nepali.

"Darjeeling has many religions, actually," said Mr. Pradhan. "We have equally large numbers of Hindus, Buddhists and Muslims, besides Christians. And I am glad to say that all live in peace with each other."

After getting down at the taxi stand near the supermarket, they walked through the crowded Chowk Bazaar. There were lots of people around the market square.

"What do you say to having lunch? I can take you to a place that serves delicious Chinese food," said Mr. Pradhan.

"Yes, let's do that!" agreed Kali's dad.

Mr. Pradhan took them to the New Dish Restaurant, which was on their way. There was an appetising aroma around the place. The man at the counter was quite fat, with a podgy but pleasant face. He welcomed them with a big smile.

They sat down inside one of the cubicles with windows facing the busy street outside and ordered Chicken Chow mein, Momos and Pork Chilly. The service was fast and the steaming food was on their table within minutes.

As promised by Mr. Pradhan, the food was really delicious as well as filling. After having coffee, they left the restaurant pleasantly full. On the way, they stopped at the red-coloured General Post Office where Kali posted some cards to her friends back home.

A little way above the Post Office, they saw a crowd gathered outside the Rink Cinema Hall. It seemed people here liked to see films in halls. "People here like to go to see films in cinema halls," Mr. Pradhan said as if answering an invisible query from his visitors.

"Are Nepali films shown much here, Raj?" asked Mr. Nepali.

"Certainly," Mr. Pradhan answered, "but of course, there are more Hindi and English films shown."

The next few days they spent visiting all the interesting places in the town. They went in the early hours to view the sunrise from Tiger Hill. They also visited Lal Durbar, which had one of the most beautiful gardens they had ever seen. One afternoon they went to Mahankal Temple up on Observatory Hill, which was above Chowrasta. Kali was surprised to see that the temple had both a Hindu and a Buddhist Priest in the temple.

On the night before Kali was to join the hostel, Mr. Pradhan gave a small party in his house and invited a few friends. Kali enjoyed watching the senior dance. Her mother was a little reluctant at first to join the dance, but at Mrs. Pradhan's insistence, danced for a while with Mr. Nepali, and then with Mr. Pradhan.

As Mr. Pradhan twirled her mum expertly around, Kali saw that her dad was dancing with Mrs. Pradhan. Kali noticed her mum cast a worried sideways glance at the couple. Kali could understand her concern, because her dad seemed to be dancing quite closely with the beautiful Mrs. Pradhan. She could see that her dad was having a really gala time!

Soon enough Mrs. Nepali had her husband sitting next to her. Kali thought that her dad looked definitely sheepish, and his expression was like that of a puppy that had been scolded. She smiled to herself; she really loved her dad so much because he was so like a little boy sometimes!

Maybe because of this side of him, he loved playing with children. In fact, this was a common trait of both Kali and her dad, and when they saw little kids while walking or shopping, they always enjoyed stopping for a few moments to play with them.

Kali and Reva also joined in the dancing and enjoyed themselves thoroughly. Ashish, although a little quiet, was busy tending to the guests, of

The Dark Mermaid

which there were twelve. He was very courteous and polite. After dinner, the guests started leaving. Soon all had left, their good byes trailing in the cold air behind them.

That night, as Kali climbed into her bed, she could hear her mum in the next room, berating her dad. She fell no end of amusement, as she knew her Dad would still have the hangdog look that his face automatically took on when his wife started her tirade.

Kali was too tired to keep her eyes open for long and as she drifted into sleep, she heard her mum say, "Did you have to dance so close with Pushpa? You didn't dance like that with me!"

And her dad says in a wounded voice, "But Mina, it was only a dance. I haven't committed a crime or anything!"

CHAPTER 9

SHIKHA AND SAMMY

The next morning all of them went to take Kali to the hostel. Today there was a big crowd of children and their parents all over the school grounds. The children were in their school uniforms and looked smart and well turned out. Kali too looked smart in her new uniform of navy blue skirt and blazer, as well as white shirt with blue and yellow striped tie. She was proud to be wearing the elegant school badge on the top pocket of her blazer.

They went up to the dormitory in the Main Building and found that Kali had been allocated a top bunk. As they put her trunk under the bed, they noticed that there was a small cupboard beside the bed. On opening it, Kali saw that it had two sections and one of them was already filled with various toiletries and clothes. Kali read the name neatly pasted on the door, 'Shikha Lamichane.'

The Dark Mermaid

"Oh, that's great Dad, my partner is a Nepali girl!" exclaimed Kali.

Just then a girl's voice spoke up behind them, "Hey, are you on the top bunk?"

Kali looked at the girl. She was fair and pretty, with shoulder-length glossy black hair. She was quite tall, almost as tall as Kali.

"Yes," Kali replied, "I'm Kali Nepali. You must be Shikha."

"Hi! Hey, how do you know my name?" Shikha asked Kali.

Kali pointed to the name on the door and Shikha exclaimed, "Of course! How silly of me to ask!"

"Hey, are we in the same class? 8B?" the pretty girl wanted to know.

"That's right, I'm in 8B," confirmed Kali.

"Superb!" exclaimed Shikha.

In answer to Mrs. Nepali's query, she informed them that she had been living in the hostel right from class one itself.

"That's nice," said Mrs. Nepali, "Now Kali, you needn't worry about anything. I'm sure Shikha will help you settle down."

"Of course I will," assured Shikha. She told them that her home was in Kathmandu and that her parents had a hotel there.

Shikha and Sammy

Shikha took them around the school premises and, pointing to the tennis court, said to Kali, "This is my favourite place."

"Oh, so you are a tennis player, are you?" Kali remarked.

"Yes, I love tennis, especially Andre Agassi!" said Shikha, with a laugh. "What's your favourite sport, Kali?"

"Swimming," Kali told her.

"I like swimming too," said Shikha, "But I am not that good. Do you swim well?"

"I swim quite well," said Kali shortly.

Her parents exchanged knowing glances. They were proud of their daughter's modesty. Shortly afterwards, they said their goodbyes. Mrs. Nepali wiped a tear as she hugged her daughter.

"We'll leave for Birganj tomorrow Kali," informed her dad. "If you need anything you can tell Reva and I'm sure Uncle Raj will take care of it."

"Yes, Kali, don't be afraid to tell me if there's anything you need," assured Mr. Pradhan.

"When will you come back to Darjeeling, Dad? Mum?" asked Kali in a small voice.

"Maybe to pick you up during the Dusshera holidays in October," answered her dad, "but we might be back sooner, who knows?"

As her parents and the Pradhans left in the Austin taxi in which they had come, Kali felt very

The Dark Mermaid

lonely all of a sudden. The realisation struck her that she was on her own now. And that she wouldn't be seeing her parents for a long time.

However, the next few days passed by in such a flurry of activities that she didn't feel lonely for long. The hostel routine was quite strictly regimented. The whistle would wake them up at 5 o'clock. By 6 o'clock, they had to finish washing as well as get dressed. From six to seven was study time for the seniors, that is, for class six and above.

After the juniors had finished their breakfast at 7 o'clock, it was time for seniors to have their breakfasts. All meals were had in the underground dining hall in the Main Building.

From 7:30 a.m. to 8:15 a.m. they had to attend chapel on the first floor.

Classes began at 8:15 a.m. Seniors had eight periods of forty minutes each while juniors had seven periods and classes ended at 2:30 p.m. There was a break from 10 a.m. to 10:15 a.m. Lunchtime was 11:00 a.m. to 12:30 p.m. for juniors and 11:50 a.m. to 12:30 p.m. for seniors.

At 3:00 p.m., tea was served along with snacks. 3:00 p.m. to 5:00 p.m. was time for games.

Studies were from 5:30 p.m. to 6:30 p.m. and dinner was from six onwards.

By 8:00 p.m., the juniors were supposed to go to bed, and the seniors, by, nine. From seven to

Shikha and Sammy

eight in the evening, there was extra study period for the seniors.

All said and done, Kali became so engrossed in adjusting to this new discipline that she forgot about missing her parents. In the class room, she sat with Shikha along the wall, near a big window. All the desks were freshly painted and were of wood. There were thirty students in her class, eighteen were boys and the rest girls. The students were mostly from all over India. There were three from Bhutan and one from Thailand. She and Shikha were the only two from Nepal in the class. There were ten day scholars, and Reva and Manisha were among them. To her dismay, Kali observed that even in such a diverse group, she was the only dark skinned student. All the rest were fair complexioned.

Kali was glad to see Reva but somehow or other found that she didn't get along particularly well with her. Anyway, Reva seemed to have a lot of friends besides her best friend, Manisha. Shikha too had quite a few friends and seemed to be quite popular. At first, Kali tried to mix up with Shikha's group, but soon noticed that they didn't reciprocate accordingly. So, Kali just hung on to Shikha, hoping that she too wouldn't neglect her. Shikha was one of the kindest souls Kali had ever encountered.

Uncle Raj taught English Literature and this was Kali's favourite subject. Moral Science was the most boring. It was about the same things repeated every other day. "One should always tell the truth, no matter what," the teacher, a Brother Gurung, would lecture and Kali would think, "But everyone knows that!"

History was an interesting subject. It was taught by a white whiskered Father whose name was Father German. He was always telling stories about great battles, brave kings and queens and about the lives of famous leaders.

Kali enjoyed Mathematics, which Shikha as well as most of the class dreaded. She failed to understand why the others disliked Maths so much. She found it interesting and challenging to solve problems. Anyway, if one knew the formulae, then one could solve most of the problems without much difficulty. However, the other students did not think so. They probably felt that if they did not abhor Maths, they would not be able to consider themselves to be normal students! It seemed fashionable to absolutely dislike Maths!

Kali did not have much trouble settling down to her studies. As far as making friends was concerned, she began to despair after some time whether she would have any other friend than Shikha.

Shikha and Sammy

In her heart of hearts, Kali refused to believe that this was due to her dark complexion. She did notice, however, that she was the darkest girl in the whole school. Her name had never been a cause of much concern in Birganj. Here, she gradually began to dislike her own name. She resented that her parents had named her so.

She tried to be extra friendly and helpful but she could not succeed in becoming intimate with any other student than Shikha. At times, she had the feeling that she was often avoided by others deliberately.

'Well, Thank God, Shikha is from Nepal. At least, we have something in common!" Kali thought gratefully.

After class hours Kali swam everyday, but here, she felt even more conscious of her dark complexion. One boy, she noticed, swam as regularly as she did. He was a bit friendlier towards her than others. Kali guessed it must be due their liking for swimming. His name was Sammy D'Costa and he was from Goa. He was in Class 8A. He, too, was of a darker complexion than most others, but not as dark as Kali.

"You swim quite well, Kali," he complimented her once.

With immense modesty, Kali replied, "I used to swim regularly in Birganj."

The Dark Mermaid

Sammy asked her, "Have you participated in competitions?"

And Kali couldn't help herself from blurting out, "Yes I have, and I have won many competitions!"

"So, you'll take part in School Competitions then?" he inquired.

"I guess I will, Sammy," agreed Kali, "When are the competitions being held?"

Sammy informed her that swimming competitions were held every year in the last week of May, and, "those who do well are selected for the Inter School Championships that are held in July."

"Well, I know I can get selected. Just wait and see," Kali boasted vainly.

Sammy looked a little doubtful and said, "I must tell you, Kali, that some of the girls in our school are pretty good. Especially, those in the upper classes."

Setting aside her modesty, Kali repeated, "Wait and see. I will win!"

"Maybe you will, Kali," Sammy cautioned her, "but, you will have to practice really hard."

From then on, Kali took extra notice of the other girls who swam regularly. They seemed to be quite proficient. Some of them were also receiving special coaching by the swimming coach. His name was Mr. Santosh Rane. He was around forty

Shikha and Sammy

years of age and had a slim build. He was from Bombay.

Although he did keep a sharp eye out on everybody in the pool, most of his coaching was confined to those who were likely to be in the School Swimming Team. He did not pay much attention to Kali. Mostly, Kali practised on her own.

It had now been quite some time since Kali had had to take her asthma medicine. Kali thanked God that she hadn't had an asthma attack for the last month or so. However, she was heedful of the doctor's advice not to overexert herself. She was fearful that her asthma might return to plague her again if she did so.

At the beginning of May, interested students were notified to submit their names if they wanted to participate in the Annual School Competitions to be held later in the month. Kali observed that there were to be two groups, junior group for Class Six and below, and Senior Group for the rest. She submitted her name for the freestyles and the backstroke.

The whole of the next week, however, they had to forget about the competitions and instead concentrate on their first term exams. Kali sailed through the exams without any problems. The questions were easy enough, because not much

The Dark Mermaid

subject matter had been covered in the first two months of study.

As soon as the exams were over, Kali began to get up early and went swimming for an hour or so. In the evening too, she put in at least two hours in the pool. At weekends, she even declined to go out in the town with Shikha because she wanted to spend the time in practice.

"I must do well in the competition, and then I will surely be more popular," thought Kali to herself.

Sometimes she raced Sammy. She could keep up with him for most of the length of the pool, but at the last few metres Sammy always managed to leave her behind.

"Come on Kali, no need to look so sad!" Sammy consoled her, "I am after all stronger than you. I'm sure you'll do much better against girls."

But of course, Kali was not easily consoled. She remembered having beaten many boys her age in Birganj.

"No, Sammy, don't say that, "she responded, "so what if I am a girl? You just wait and see! One day I'll surely beat you." She sounded very confident.

"Don't be so sure," Sammy was a bit put off by her overconfidence.

"Oh, if only you were to know about how I used to beat most of the boys in Birganj!" Kali said to

Shikha and Sammy

herself wistfully. However, she didn't want to boast anymore and lose even the few friends she had! Of course, Kali thought she was as good as ready. She felt strong and sure of herself.

As she was thinking all this, Shikha came over to the side of the pool and informed her friend excitedly, "Kali, do you know that our class is going to Loyd's Botanical Gardens tomorrow?"

"What for, Shikha?" asked Sammy. "Is my class going too?"

"No, it's only 8B," Shikha explained, "and it's for half a day! Mr. Gomes is taking us." Mr. Gomes was the biology teacher.

Thankfully, the next day was full of bright sunshine as they left for the garden. The Lloyd's Botanical Garden was located near Loreto Convent, and was a few kilometres from Mount Hermon. As soon as they entered the moss-covered gates, Kali was enthralled. She had never been to such a garden! It was spread around many acres of land. The small hillocks and slopes were full of sumptuous green grass and all along the narrow pebbled paths were rows of flowers.

In many places, one could see groups of plants with many coloured flowers. They visited the huge greenhouse that had thousands of potted plants inside. There was a fountain in the middle and Kali could see a lot of goldfish swimming around in

The Dark Mermaid

the pool. Kali was simply amazed at the variety of flowers in the garden. And there were so many different types of cactus plants!

Mr. Gomes, the biology teacher, lead them around and asked them to read the scientific names as well as the common names of the plants. He also showed them trees that were very old. Time passed very fast and before they knew it, it was time to go back to school. They lined up to walk back to the bus parked outside the gates.

Getting in line, Shikha showed Kali a purple-coloured flower and whispered, "Kali, look at this flower, it smells really nice!"

"Let me see." Kali took the flower and holding it close to her nose, took a deep sniff. "You are right, Shikha, it smells so nice!" So saying, she again put it to her nose.

Alas! How could she know that the lovely smell of the purple flower would be the cause of her downfall!

CHAPTER 10
THE COMPETITION

That very night, Kali had an asthmatic attack. Even after taking her medicine, she couldn't sleep for a long time. She tossed around on her bed late into the night. In the morning, she awoke with great difficulty, feeling very drowsy. She couldn't practice in the morning. In class, she had a hard time concentrating on what was being taught.

"What's the matter, Kali? You don't look your usual self," observed Shikha.

Kali replied that she hadn't slept well that night.

During lunch, Sammy also inquired, "Kali, you didn't practice swimming today. What's the matter, aren't you well?"

"I'm all right, Sammy," replied Kali, "It's just that I had difficulty sleeping last night."

"Well then, you'd better practice extra hours this evening. The other girls were all there this morning," advised Sammy.

"Sure, Sammy, and thanks for your concern," Kali replied. But she was worried that perhaps, she wouldn't be able to practice that evening either. She still felt a tightness in her chest. She took her medicine during the lunch break. By the end of class hours, she felt sufficiently better to venture into the pool. However, after a few minutes of swimming, she found herself wheezing and gasping for breath.

She stood to the side to take some rest and wait for her breathing to come back to normal. She wondered whether it was because of the outing yesterday that her asthma had returned to torture her. She had read in a medical book in her father's study that pollen grains were a common cause of asthmatic attacks. Since it was the spring season, it was possible that the Botanical Gardens, where they had gone yesterday, must have had plenty of pollen all over the place. She remembered sniffing the beautiful purple flower and now really regretted doing so.

She didn't want to tell anybody that she had asthma. She was afraid that the coach would find out and stop her from competing.

"Oh well, plenty of people have lots of sicknesses, but still many of them compete and even become champions," Kali consoled herself.

The Competition

She remembered one American girl who had won swimming gold medals in the Olympics some years back. She had later revealed that she had always had asthma, right from childhood. In fact, she admitted that during childhood, she would have asthma attacks even at the slightest exertion, like climbing stairs of her home.

Thinking about this brave girl gave Kali renewed vigour. She started practising with new determination. That night she had a good night's sleep. She awoke refreshed in the early morning and met Sammy and the other girls at the pool. Since the heats were to take place the next day, they didn't practice too hard. They needed to save their energy for the actual competitions.

"If you ask me, Kali, I think Soni will be tough to beat in the freestyles. And I think Hita will be the one to watch out for in the backstroke," was Sammy's opinion.

Kali looked at the two girls, who were swimming at a leisurely pace. They were from Class Eight and both were tall and strongly built. Hita looked especially strong.

Kali had to admit that they would be worthy competitors.

"Sammy," she remarked, however, "That's your opinion. If you ask me, I think they aren't that fast. I have watched them swim."

The Dark Mermaid

"Well, we'll know tomorrow, won't we?" Sammy replied, sounding a bit piqued.

Mr. Santosh Rane, as usual, was giving them a lot of instructions like, "Girls, don't splash the water so much." "Soni, stretch out your legs more, you aren't bending your arms enough." "Hita, keep your head still!"

Kali smiled to herself. If her father had been present, he would surely have been instructing them to tuck in their chins. That was his favourite line as far as coaching was concerned!

That evening Kali had a hearty dinner and went to bed early. She prayed that she wouldn't be troubled by asthma that night. But, as usual, fate had other ideas for her. At around two in the night, she woke up feeling breathless. She took a few deep breaths but it didn't help much. Her breathing became heavy and with every laboured breath, a wheezing sound escaped her lips.

Kali got up and took one tablet of her medicine. She tried to go back to sleep. She was, however, much troubled. Even after her breathing had become a bit easier, she tossed and turned on her bed. It was far from the restful sleep she needed to be prepared for the day's competitions.

"Oh Lord, why have you done this?" she asked God, " please help me, God, please let me win in the heats and qualify for the final competitions!"

The Competition

She felt very tired and listless as she joined Shikha for breakfast in the dining hall. There was a lot of excited chatter all around the tables. Everyone was looking forward to the heats, which began at ten o'clock.

"Here Kali, have one more omelette, you'll need it," said Shikha.

"Thanks, Shikha, " said Kali.

Kali tried to act normal and as excited as everybody else, but in spite of the brave front, she was very afraid.

"If I overexert myself I'll get an asthmatic attack. Then everyone will know," thought Kali, "and I won't be permitted to compete."

Driven by such thoughts, Kali went to the dormitory and took out another tablet of her medicine from the cupboard. She looked at the small white tablet and thought, "I think I'll take one tablet right now. Then, maybe I will be all right." She gulped it down with water and went to the pool.

The first heats were for the older group of swimmers. She saw that this group was divided into three groups of five each. The three winners, as well as the two best-placed seconds in the heats, would qualify for the finals. There were to be eight events. Kali was especially interested in the freestyles and backstrokes. Shortly, it was time for

The Dark Mermaid

Kali and her group to take their places at the starting blocks.

Loosening her shoulders and shaking her legs, she took some deep breaths. She still didn't feel too good about her breathing. But now, there was no time to think about it. The coach had already shouted out his command for them to be ready.

"Get set", he called out, and as the five competitors crouched in their positions, "Go!"

As was her usual habit, Kali dived in a bit clumsily, while all the others dived in smoothly. This was the freestyle event over 100 metres, that is twice the length of the pool. There would be two laps. Kali was the third to touch the first fifty-metre mark and to turn around for the next lap.

She was well into her rhythm and she started now to put in extra effort in her movements, with the result that a small frothing wake formed behind her as her legs kicked the water violently. Now, she was ahead of the others and only about ten metres remained to the finish. Kali felt a burst of exultation, but the very next moment a wrenching feeling clasped her chest. She faltered in her movements. Her chest tightened. She could hardly breathe. Two girls overtook her and Kali could only watch helplessly as they touched the finish line ahead of her.

The Competition

With a deep sense of gloom, Kali pulled herself out of the water. She was breathless and was wheezing. She knew that she hadn't qualified for the finals. As she walked despondently towards the dressing room, Shikha came up to her and consoled her, "It's okay, Kali, you almost won the race. It's only bad luck."

"If only you knew, Shikha," Kali said to herself, "but I can't even tell you about my problem. I don't want anybody to know, otherwise I will never be given a chance to compete again."

In the shower, she took deep breaths and couldn't help herself from shedding a few tears. Of course, she wouldn't let anybody else see her crying. She was too proud for that. At the same time she cursed her luck. Why did I have to get asthmatic attack so near the competitions?

"As it is, God, nobody likes me. If I don't do well in swimming, I'll never be able to prove that I am worth anything," she implored the heavens. "So my good Lord, please, please, help me win the backstroke at least!"

Kali constantly talked to God and always felt better after doing so. But there had been times when she had thought that God wasn't listening to her. This had been her view especially in the last few months when she had started to have her attacks, and couldn't even run around with friends.

The Dark Mermaid

She had also been especially remorseful towards God when at night she couldn't sleep at all because of breathing troubles. But no matter how resentful she felt, she always ended up by praying, "Oh God, I thank you for all you have done for me. I thank you for giving me loving parents. Please keep them safe and healthy. Oh Lord, please help me also. Give me good health. Please get rid of my asthma problem!"

Although she felt much better after praying, it didn't get rid of her problem. However, Kali was old enough and wise enough to know that there were worse-off people in the world. There were so many kids on the streets who didn't have anybody to look after them. She had often seen kids in tattered clothes and dirty tangled hair, scavenging stinking rubbish at roadsides and in rubbish containers. Kali had also seen blind and lame people begging outside many temples. Compared to them, she felt herself to be lucky.

Sitting on a bench in the dressing room, Kali was thinking of all this, when Shikha came scampering in to inform her that the next event would be the backstroke. She also wanted to know, "By the way, Kali, why didn't you come to watch Sammy race? He won both his events."

Kali was glad to hear this. After all, Sammy was her only friend besides Shikha in the school.

The Competition

However, she also felt a sense of gloom. There was still a slight wheezing sound in her chest. Her breathing was ragged. In addition, she didn't have much confidence in herself anymore.

Of course, she had no choice other than to take part in the backstroke event. It never crossed her mind that she could withdraw from the race. She had way too much courage for that!

Right from the start, she trailed behind all the others. To keep some of her bedraggled dignity intact, she tried in the last ten metres to swim faster, though the pain in her chest was agonising. She didn't want to be last, no matter what. She finished in the third position again. This time Sammy pulled her up and said a few kind words about there always being a next time.

Kali kept her head up and thanked him graciously. Inside, she felt like crying.

That night Kali didn't even pray, she felt so depressed.

"Why did I have to get asthma? I couldn't even qualify for the finals. What must Sammy and the others be thinking?" she said to herself again and again.

And she remembered, "I had told them about being a champion in my hometown. Now they must be thinking that I was lying. What will they think of me now?"

She blamed herself mercilessly.

CHAPTER 11
LEARNING TO BREATHE

The following days were despondent ones for Kali. Somehow, from the very next day after the competition, Kali was free of asthma problems. This continued to be so in the following weeks too.

She had watched the finals with disinterest, her mind full of resentment. Sammy had won in three events, the 50 and 100 metre freestyles and the relay. In the other groups, the races had been closely contested and quite exciting. Soni had won the 100 metre freestyle and Hita had won the 100 metres backstroke as expected.

All through the competitions Kali kept thinking, "How I wish I was competing. Now I will never swim again. I'll never be able to win any race."

In addition, she imagined that some of her schoolmates must be ridiculing her. One or two of them did offer some consolatory words. After the races, Soni and Hita had come up to her. Both had said words of sympathy, which actually made Kali feel all the worse.

Mr. Santosh Rane, the coach, had patted her encouragingly on her back and said, "Kali, you didn't do so badly. You might not have been used to racing at high altitude. In time, you will get used to it and I'm sure you will do better."

In the following weeks, she gradually began to forget about her ill luck. She went back to being her warm and friendly self. She wrote a letter to her parents telling them only that she had not won any races in the swimming competition. Her father wrote back asking her to take her medicines regularly. He further advised her to keep on swimming, but not to overexert herself.

Kali could imagine that her dad must have been quite disappointed to hear about her losing. He must also have guessed at the real reason for her poor performance. Although he did not say so in his letter, Kali was sure he knew.

"That's why he has asked me to take my medicines regularly," she guessed.

Kali felt especially bad that she couldn't talk about her problem with anybody. However, she was soon back to her usual routine of swimming in the morning and in the evenings. She thought every night about when she would be able to race again. Kali was a very competitive girl, if nothing else.

The Dark Mermaid

In July, the prestigious Inter School Championships would be held.

"You know, Mount Hermon has always done well in swimming," Sammy had told her, "Last year, we did quite badly. We only came third. Before that we were champions for two years consecutively."

"Who won?" Kali asked.

"Dr. Graham's Homes of Kalimpong won the championships," replied Sammy, "Goethals of Kurseong came second."

"What about the other schools of Darjeeling?" enquired Kali, "Aren't they any good?"

"Well, actually St. Joseph's and St. Paul's are not very good." He answered, "St. Joseph's is very good in football and are the champions. And St. Paul's is good in cricket. They are more interested in those sports than in swimming."

"I didn't know that," said Kali, "I had thought that St. Joseph's would be good. I had heard about their brand new indoor heated swimming pool."

"Yes, you're right. They might be good in a few years time. Of course, you know that all school swimming pools are heated. Otherwise we couldn't swim for half the year! Anyway, we have to do really well this year," said Sammy, "You see, swimming is what Mount Hermon is good at. It's a matter of honour, Kali!"

Learning to Breathe

That night Kali dreamt that she had been selected to compete in the Inter School Championships and that she had done her school proud by winning in the freestyles and the backstroke. In her dream, she saw herself helping her school win the prestigious relay race. She saw herself standing on the winner's podium and having the gold medals put around her neck. All the others students came up to congratulate her, the seniors hearty in their approval, and the juniors looking at her in awe.

That morning she woke up feeling very refreshed and happy.

"What a nice dream!" she thought.

That day she went for morning practice in the pool with an extra spring in her step. She knew very well that she wouldn't be participating in the coming Inter School Championships, but that did not deter her from practising as if she were really going to.

"Who knows?" she had remarked to Shikha once when her friend had commented that she didn't know why Kali was practising so hard, "You know, you can't compete this year."

"Who knows?" she had repeated, "Maybe the coach might realise that I am good and decide to make me compete."

Kali was an optimistic girl and she somehow held the hope that she would be asked to take part

The Dark Mermaid

in the championships. She didn't know how it could be possible, but still she didn't let her hopes die. Deep inside, she knew that she was much faster than the other girls in her school team. She just hadn't been able to show her potential.

"I wish Dad was here to advise me," she thought wistfully. "He would have been such a great help."

Of course, she knew it would not be possible for him to come, as he would be busy with work. And Kali knew that in this she really was all alone. She kept on hoping, especially since she hadn't had any breathing problems for a long time now.

"It's quite miraculous," she found herself thinking.

"Well, not so miraculous," she corrected herself. "Thank God I found that book in the library which explained how people with asthma problems could have healthier lives.

The book, titled 'Exercises Asthmatics must do' was written by some doctor. She had gone through it with great interest. She had learnt that there were some special kinds of breathing exercises that would help asthmatic patients live a normal life. The exercises were explained in detail with a lot of step-by-step pictures.

Kali had practised them in secret. She had almost mastered a few of them. They weren't so

Learning to Breathe

difficult to do. One of them, she found particularly to her liking. This exercise told her to lie down on her bed with her legs straight and her arms limp by her sides. She had to breathe in deeply through her nose. While doing so, she was to expand her stomach out fully. Then, immediately she had to expand her chest as much as possible.

At this point, she was supposed to hold her breath and count slowly to eight. After this she had to contract her abdomen in tightly and push the breath out through her mouth. Kali learnt that by holding her breath for eight counts while her stomach and chest were expanded, all the oxygen would be fully utilised. Then, when she expelled her breath out by pulling her stomach in, she would be forcing out de-oxygenated air completely from her body.

The first few times she did the exercise, she found it hard to hold her breath for the full eight counts. However, after many attempts, she had no problem doing so. Sometimes Kali also felt a little giddy and light-headed after repeating the exercise a couple of times. But always she felt refreshed with new energy.

"It's quite exhilarating," she thought to herself.

It was also convenient that she could do it lying down. She could do it on her bed in the morning

The Dark Mermaid

and at night, without any one knowing about it. She could also do it on her feet, in which case she had to move her arms in circling movements that made it seem as if she was doing some martial arts exercise.

There were also other exercises she learnt, but this was her favourite. Gradually it became a habit to be doing the exercise even in class. Sometimes, she herself would not be aware that she was doing it! In addition to this, Kali had also read in the book that asthmatics should not do any heavy activities without first warming up thoroughly. Thus, she had taken to jogging around the football field early mornings. At first, she jogged at a slow pace and only for a few laps. However, as her confidence grew, she was soon running faster and ten laps of the 400 metres field was not posing any great problems.

After running, she often took her pulse rate and found to her delight that it would not be racing even after ten laps. After this she would go to the pool. Here, too, she never went in without first doing some stretching exercises. She did, at times, feel impatient to get into the water, but her determination to make herself completely fit, stopped her from doing so.

In the pool, she always did a few laps at a very leisurely pace and only then did she start to race against herself.

Learning to Breathe

In a month's time, Kali had developed better stamina than she had ever been able to.

"Citrus foods like oranges can cause attacks, as can strong scents like that of fresh paint," was on page ten of the book.

"It is also advisable to refrain from eating too much fish," was on page eleven.

Chapter four told her to have a positive outlook towards life. She should divert her mind to other things, rather than always thinking about her own problems. Kali was really glad to have found such an important book. It was indeed very helpful.

"I really must read more books," she said to Shikha. "One can learn so many new things."

Shikha was delighted to hear Kali say so. She herself was an avid reader and spent a considerable time in the school library. In fact, her constant complaint was that the library didn't have enough books!

"So glad to hear that," she responded happily. "Now, we will have a common interest."

One day, as they were coming out of the library, Shikha quipped, "Kali, you should read Mills and Boons novels. They are so romantic!"

"I think, I'll just go through health and sports books for the moment." Kali didn't much fancy the mushy stuff in some romantic books she had skimmed through.

The Dark Mermaid

"Oh, you should read about the tall, dark and handsome heroes! Mills and Boon is what I like," enthused Shikha, "and Mills and Boon is what I'll read!"

Well, each to her own, thought Kali. However, she decided to read a Mills and Boon some day to see what it was that Shikha was so enamoured with!

The increased visits to the library gave her new knowledge. Like the breathing exercises, Kali had also read about physical ones. She read, much to her delight, that there were plenty of young swimmers her age, who had broken world records. Some had even won in the Olympics!

Kali herself had many a time dreamt about winning an Olympic medal.

She had found an especially informative book called 'The History of Swimming'. From it she found out that Ilsa Korals of Australia, at age 13, had set the 800-metre world record in 1958. In 1964, another 13-year-old girl from the United States, Patty Carreto, became the world 1500-metre record holder. Similarly, in 1966, Irina Pozdyakova, aged 13, had set a new world record in the 200-metre breaststroke.

Inge Sorensen, a 12-year-old from Denmark, had won a bronze in the 200-metre breaststroke at the Berlin Olympics. In the Los Angeles Olympics, a 14-year-old Japanese girl, Kusuo Kitamura, had won in the 1500 metres. At the same Olympics, 14-year-old Willie den Ouden of Holland, had won a silver in the 100 metres.

Kali learned that young girls her age had very good chances of becoming world champions in middle distance races. This was because, in such races, buoyancy and lung capacity were more important than strength only. The youngsters had good lung capacity in proportion to their light body weights. However, Kali learnt, in the shorter races like 50 metres and 100 metres, the older girls had a definite advantage, due to their superior strength. And, Kali knew, strength meant power.

This was why Kali was spending regular time at the gym, where she asked Sammy to help her do weight training. She trained with light weights, but repeatedly, so that in a few weeks time her shoulders and arms were much stronger without her gaining much weight.

"You are looking good," Shikha remarked to her as they were going to class, "What's the secret?"

Kali smiled and said jokingly, "Weight training, Shikha. Why don't you try it?"

She knew very well that pretty and delicate Shikha would never, for the life of her, venture into the gym.

The Dark Mermaid

As if reading her thoughts, Shikha exclaimed, "My God, Kali, how can you stand the smell in the gym? It stinks." She wrinkled her pert nose.

"That's so, "Kali admitted. But she didn't mention that she herself liked the smell of perspiration as she did her training in the gym. "The more the smell," she thought, "the better the exercises."

It was the first day of July and there was a heavy shower. The monsoon had started. They went into the main building of the school. As they entered the corridor, Kali saw a crowd in front of the notice board. As she came closer, she saw that there was a big poster with a picture of a swimmer about to dive into a pool.

She heard an excited murmuring in the crowd. Sammy was also there and his face too was alight with excitement. Pushing through the crowd, Kali looked up at the poster.

It read: -

7th Inter School Swimming Championships
Date: 15th July
Venue: —St. Joseph's School, North Point, Darjeeling.
Participants:
1. Dr. Graham's Homes, Kalimpong
2. Goethal's Memorial School, Kurseong
3. Mount Hermon School, Darjeeling

4. St. Paul's School (boys), Darjeeling and Loreto Convent (girls), Darjeeling—Combined Team

5. Mirik Co educational, Mirik

6. Daffodil's Co-educational, Kalimpong

7. Victoria Boys School (boys), Kurseong and St. Helen's Girls School (girls), Kurseong—Combined Team

8. St. Augustine's School, Kurseong

9. St. Robert's School (Boys), Darjeeling and St. Teresa's Girls School (girls), Darjeeling—Combined Team

10. St. Joseph's School (boys), Darjeeling and St. Joseph's Convent (girls), Kalimpong—Combined team

Events:

1. 50 metres Freestyle for boys and girls
2. 100 metres Freestyle for boys and girls
3. 100 metres Butterfly for boys and girls
4. 100 metres Breaststroke for boys and girls
5. 100 metres Backstroke for boys and girls
6. 4x100 metres Relay for Boys
7. 4x100 metres Relay for Girls

At the bottom of the poster there was a special notice in bold letters:

The Dark Mermaid
SPECIAL NOTICE

For the first time, a "Swimmer of the Year" award will be presented to the competitor adjudged the best swimmer in the Championships. The prize will include a handsome trophy and a cash award of Rs. 10,000.00. There will be only one such award. There will not be separate awards for boys and girls.

CHAPTER 12

HOPING FOR A MIRACLE

'Outstanding Swimmer of the Year'! Kali's eyes stayed glued to the words.

"I know I could win that title. Oh, how proud my dad would be!" she thought wistfully.

She also knew that if she could win this prize, she would be popular with her schoolmates. In fact, Kali now was convinced that this was the only way she could be really accepted by the others in the school. Her overtures of friendship had got her nowhere.

Lost in such thoughts, she didn't notice that Sammy was tapping her on the shoulder, until he had to shout in her ears, "Hey, Kali, what's the matter with you?"

"Oh, sorry," said Kali. "Actually I was reading the announcement. You might win the best swimmer award, Sammy. Of course, you will have to put in a lot of extra effort, I think."

"Oh, really?" replied Sammy, "I didn't know you were such an expert. Anyway, Kali, you should know that the other schools have some pretty fast swimmers in their teams."

"Well, I do hope our school wins the championships," she said.

"It won't be easy, Kali," Sammy said seriously. "You see, we don't have any really good swimmers this year."

If I was in the team, we could win, said Kali to herself. She kept her thoughts to herself. It wouldn't have sounded nice, not after she had failed to even qualify for the School Championships.

That night she prayed extra hard, "Oh, Dear God, I know you love me. And even though I have been cursed with bad luck, I know you will forgive me if I have committed any sins. Please get rid of my asthma, so that I can be a swimming champion someday."

Before closing her eyes, Kali prayed again to somehow give her the chance to compete in the Inter School Championships.

She slept fitfully that night and had the same dream about winning many of the races and standing on the winner's podium and being awarded the Swimmer of the Year prize.

However, today she woke up before she could get her medals.

Hoping for a Miracle

In the morning, she strolled over to the pool to watch the school team practice. Today Mr. Rane was very busy, shouting instructions left and right. Kali could understand that he must be quite worried, as they had not at all done well the year before. He had been school coach for the last five years, and, although his team had won twice during this time, the year before had been a big disappointment.

He certainly didn't want to repeat it. Therefore, he was acting like a really tough coach today.

Soni, Kali could see, was almost in tears. She had received a really big bawling out for not moving her arms fast enough.

Kali watched Sammy and the other boys race each other. Sammy was the fastest of the lot, the others were not so fast, Kali thought. Soni and Hita were quite good, but as far as the others were concerned, it was not difficult to see that they weren't very fast either. Except maybe for the girl who would be racing in the 50-metre butterfly, and whose name was Sita.

"I know, I could win the 50 and 100 metre freestyles," thought Kali, "I could also have a good chance in the backstroke if I tried hard enough."

All this was, of course, wishful thinking. The team had already been selected. Soni, Hita, Neema, Sita and Romi would make up the girls' team while

The Dark Mermaid

the boys' team consisted of Sammy, Jigmy, Palten, Raju and Amitav.

In class, Kali had difficulty in concentrating in what was being taught.

"Kali, I have been noticing that you are not concentrating on your lessons. Your mind seems to be elsewhere," Mr. Raj Pradhan pointed out once when she had gone to visit them during a weekend.

"Oh, don't do that, Raj," pretty Mrs. Pradhan rebuked her husband. "Poor Kali is here on holiday."

"No, Auntie," Kali admitted, "Uncle Raj is right. I must pay more attention in class. Don't worry, Uncle, I will."

"That's fine then," Mr. Pradhan put the subject aside. "Now, where have Ashish and Reva gone?"

"Oh, they will be here shortly," replied his wife.

"Let them come. We will all go horse riding. How's that, Kali?" asked Mr. Pradhan more kindly.

"Of course, that's fantastic, Uncle," said Kali.

However, Kali knew that until the Inter School Championships were over, she wouldn't be able to enjoy horse riding or even pay much attention in class. She kept such thoughts to herself.

That evening Kali decided to go to the pool when it was empty. She wanted to satisfy herself that she still had the potential to be a champion.

Hoping for a Miracle

She wanted to swim as fast as she could and to time herself over different distances.

She was too shy and nervous to do so in front of others.

"I never know when I will have breathing problems!" she thought.

She waited until there was no one left in the pool. Quickly she changed into her black one-piece swimsuit, and, tucking her hair beneath a black swimming cap, jumped into the cool waters. She shivered slightly, although she knew the water had been heated just a while ago. She had come to know that the schools in Darjeeling had heated swimming pools. Otherwise no, one would have been able to swim for almost half the year!

She began to swim at a snail's pace, remembering the lesson she had learnt from the exercise book. She gradually built up her speed. After a while, she took her position at one end of the pool, and taking a deep breath, dived in and started to race herself over 50 metres, then over 100 metres. After resting awhile, she swam the backstroke over 100 metres, at full speed again.

She timed herself on her special waterproof watch, the one her dad had given on her last birthday. It also functioned as a stopwatch and was very accurate. She found her timings in all the

The Dark Mermaid

distances to be good. In the backstroke, it was quite outstanding! She couldn't believe it at first.

"Wow! It's almost the same as the South Asian Record!" she exulted to herself.

Kali knew most of the swimming records of the world. Her knowledge had been further increased by reading the books in the school library. For instance, she knew that the world record in 50 metre freestyle was 0:24:13, set by Inge de Brunje of Holland and she had also set the record in the 100 metre freestyle at 0:53:77.

In the 50 metre backstroke, Sandra Voelker of Germany had set the world record at 0:28:25, while in the 100 metre backstroke, Natalie Couglin of United States had set the world record at 0:59:58.

"Of course, I am a long way from such records," Kali thought, "but still, my timings are not that bad either!"

With a feeling of satisfaction, Kali got out of the pool. She was very pleased with herself and had regained some of her lost confidence. As she walked away from the pool, a shadowy figure walked out from behind a tree.

CHAPTER 13

THE SURPRISE

He was holding a stopwatch. He looked at the back of the departing girl, his face showed some disbelief. Curiosity at seeing a lone girl swimming alone in the late evening had made Mr. Santosh Rane watch for some time.

"Who could it be, swimming all alone at this late hour?" he had asked himself.

He had watched Kali compete the first freestyle over 50 metres. He had guessed that the timing must have been pretty good. This had made him take out his ever-present stopwatch. He had timed the 100-metre freestyle. He had been more than a little surprised. The timing was excellent, better than any of the other girls in the School Team. In fact, it was quite close to the Inter School record set by one of his own students almost five years ago. It had not yet been broken.

The Dark Mermaid

"This girl can break that record, I am sure," he guessed.

The backstroke was even better. The girl swam the backstroke really well. Her head was dead still and she swam in a very straight line. Her arms moved efficiently, cutting the water in beautiful rapid strokes. He had also noticed that when she had been swimming freestyle, the girl's feet paddled so rapidly that they seemed to be fast moving pistons.

"I wish this girl was in my team," he thought, "but I can't have her on the team now."

He remembered now that the girl's name was Kali, and that she had failed to qualify in the school competitions.

"She had started well, but couldn't finish as well," he remembered. "I wonder what happened to her that day?"

He went back to his room, deep in thought.

The next morning he went to talk to the Principal, Mr. D'Souza.

"Come in, Mr. Rane," the Principal invited the swimming coach in. "Anything particular you wanted to see me about?"

Mr. Santosh Rane, in one of the few moments in his life, was feeling very awkward indeed. He cleared his throat nervously. He really did not

The Surprise

know how to request the principal to allow him permission to break school rules.

Seeing his awkwardness, Mr. D'Souza said in a kind tone, "Mr. Rane, would you like a cup of tea before we discuss what's on your mind?" He had been a principal for long enough to know that even teachers and coaches sometimes acted like students. He understood many things without having everything spelled out to him. He correctly assumed that the swimming coach must be feeling quite jittery about the upcoming Inter School Championships, due soon. He probably wanted to talk about it.

"Poor chap," he said to himself, "losing last year, and not even being able to get second place, must have really disappointed him. Surely, he must have a heavy burden on his shoulders right now!"

Gratefully, Mr Rane said, "Thank you Sir, a cup of tea will be fine."

He needed some time to think of a way to put forward his unusual request.

As they sipped tea, brought in by Mr. James, the Nepali attendant, Mr. D'Souza gently swung the conversation towards the upcoming championships.

"So Coach, how is our team shaping up? Do you think they will do well this year?" he asked.

The Dark Mermaid

The coach replied, not too confidently, it seemed to the principal, "Oh yes, Sir, they are practising really hard. But I have heard that some of the other schools have some excellent swimmers in their teams this year."

"That's to be expected, Coach," said Mr. D'Souza, "but I do think that you are one of the better coaches around here. After all your teams did win previous contests."

"Thank you, Sir," Mr. Rane was pleased to hear the compliment.

"And how I need this kind of encouragement!" he said to himself, "As it is, our team really is not good enough to win the championships. But how can I admit that?"

To the principal, however, he said, "Sir, we will try our best, that's for sure. I am confident that with some luck we can be champions again."

"Well, I do think luck is important, Coach," the principal remarked, "but I believe hard work and talent is more important, don't you agree?"

The coach at last had got an opening.

"Well, Sir, you are absolutely right," he replied, "hard work is, of course, a must. At the same time, the one who does the hard work also has to have talent."

"So? Our swimmers have talent, don't they, Coach?" asked the principal.

The Surprise

"No doubt, Sir," Mr. Rane answered, "all of them have a bit of talent. But I must admit that outstanding talent is somehow lacking in the team this year."

"You mean, someone like Mae Jong? The Chinese girl from our school four, five years ago?" queried Mr. D'Souza. "She broke the record in some event, didn't she?"

"Yes, Sir, and that record is still unbroken," replied the coach, "but this year there are no girls like her in our team."

"How about the boys?" asked the principal. "What are their chances?"

"They are practising extra hard, but again, except for one or two, they are only just above average in my opinion," replied the coach.

"Then this year it will be hard going, is that what you mean, Coach?" Mr. D'Souza was not at all happy. Just the week before, he had met some colleagues from other schools at an educational meet, and he remembered boasting about his school's excellent swimming record.

"Well, Sir, actually we could win the championships this year too," Mr. Rane offered warily.

"How's that, Coach?" asked the principal, leaning forward with interest.

"Well Sir," Mr. Rane paused a while and Mr. D'Souza had to prod him with, "What? What? Come on Mr. Rane, if there is a way, let me know about it."

The Dark Mermaid

"Well, Sir," repeated Mr. Rane, a little more confidently, "You see, there is a girl in this school. She is from Nepal. Her name is Kali..."

"What about her?" asked the principal impatiently, "I know the girl."

"Well, Sir, she is not in the team. You see, she didn't qualify in the school competitions. I saw her swimming yesterday and I even timed her," he said hesitantly. He was about to say something for which the principal could very well admonish him. "She's really outstanding, Sir!"

"But you just mentioned that she hasn't qualified. How then can she be of help, Coach?" asked the principal, puzzled.

"I was wondering, you know, Sir, I was wondering," Mr. Rane faltered. His face was flushed. He pushed himself up in the chair and cleared his throat.

The principal could see that his swimming coach was very nervous indeed!

"What is it actually you were wondering about, Mr. Rane?" asked Mr. D'Souza, a bit suspiciously, it seemed to Mr. Rane!

Mr. Rane, with all the courage he could muster, blurted out, "Sir, would it be possible to include Kali in the team?"

The principal was quiet.

The Surprise

Mr. Santosh Rane added quickly, "You know, Sir, if there is any way at all that I could be allowed to have her in the team, I would be sure that we could win."

Thoughtfully Mr. D'Souza looked at Mr. Rane. After a moment he said, "Coach, I understand your difficulty. God alone knows I too have had to face some very difficult circumstances in my life. But you must know that what you wish for is impossible."

"I know, Sir," replied Mr. Rane, "I was just thinking of the good of our school. I know the rules very well. Rules are rules. However, sometimes there are ways to deal with such things."

"I don't know what you have in mind, Mr. Rane," said Mr. D'Souza, "but as far as I am concerned, it is out of the question. I think it would be better for those in the team to practice all the harder."

So saying, the Principal closed the subject. He was very strict as far as rules were concerned.

Mr. Rane gave one more try. "Sir, couldn't Kali be included as an extra swimmer?"

"No, Coach, there is no provision for such. I am sorry, and I think it would be better not to bring up this subject again."

There was a note of finality in his voice.

The Dark Mermaid

Woefully, Mr. Santosh Rane got up and bidding goodbye, took his leave.

CHAPTER 14

FEVER

Balmy weather had set in and there was a chill in the morning air. Many of the students were showing signs of having a cold. Kali took care to dress more warmly, especially as she was swimming regularly. Evening swimming was now allowed only for an hour, and the pool became more crowded than usual in the morning hours. However, a week before the Inter School Championships, the school team was given two hours off every day during the afternoon so that they could put in extra practice.

Since she wasn't in the school team, Kali practised extra hard in the mornings. She jogged around the playing field at a faster pace now and could do ten laps without difficulty. Her breathing had improved considerably. The balmy weather, combined with her regular exercises, had probably contributed to improving her health. She had had no asthmatic attacks for the whole of the last month.

Once, during her morning practice in the pool, the coach had spoke to her, "You know, Kali, I think you have the potential to be a winner."

Kali had been delighted at having been noticed by the coach.

She had replied, "Sir, I'll qualify next year and then I can take part in the Inter School."

"To tell you the truth, Kali, I wish you were in the team this year," Mr. Rane had said wistfully.

"Well, Sir, I didn't qualify, so I guess I will have to wait until next year," Kali said.

"You are right, Kali," the coach admitted, "you keep on practising regularly. After the Championships, I will give you some extra coaching."

Kali was grateful for the kind and encouraging words. And even if she was resigned to wait one whole year, she was very sad not to have qualified this year itself. However, as if to lift her spirit, she found herself doing quite well in studies.

The term results had placed her among the top ten in the class. She had done especially well in English Literature and Mathematics. Shikha too was in the top ten, whereas Reva, Uncle Raj's daughter and her best friend, Manisha, hadn't done as well.

Fever

"They don't need to," Kali thought enviously, "they are both so fair and pretty. Everybody likes them."

As the days drew closer to the Inter School Championships, there was a sense of excitement in the whole school. Students from class seven to eleven would be going to watch the competitions. Some of the older girls were more excited at the opportunity to meet boys from other schools than about the swimming contests! And the same thing applied to some of the boys.

Two days before the big event, Shikha and a lot of girls from the dormitory had to visit the infirmary for cold and flu. It seemed that a viral influenza was running through the hostel. Kali herself was not at all affected by the virus.

"Must be because of all my exercises," she said to Shikha.

All the swimmers in the team seemed to be all right, although the Coach was a worried man. Both the boys and the girl swimmers were made to sleep in the school guestrooms as a precaution.

Finally, only a day remained for the competitions. They would be going to St. Paul's School by bus at eight, the next morning. The competitions would be starting at nine sharp. The teams from Kalimpong and Kurseong had already arrived in Darjeeling.

The Dark Mermaid

Kali woke up early. Shikha, on the lower bunk, was fast asleep. She didn't look well, and had coughed throughout the night. Kali didn't think she would be going. A lot of other girls wouldn't be going either. Funnily, the virus had struck only the girls' dormitory, and there were hardly any cases of cold among the boys.

By eight, Kali had finished her breakfast and was raring to be off to St. Paul's. Reva and Manisha would be there, as would many other day scholars. As she was walking out of the dining hall with a snivelling Shikha, Kali was surprised to see Mr. Santosh Rane walking towards them an air of purpose.

"Wonder why he isn't with the team," Kali wondered out aloud, "by now, they should have started off." She knew that they would have to warm up on reaching St. Paul's. The air today was noticeably cooler.

"Kali!" shouted Mr. Rane from some distance away, "Wait, there's something I have to tell you."

Shikha looked surprised, "I wonder what he wants to tell you, Kali. Have you done something wrong?"

"No, Shikha," replied Kali, "nothing that I know of!"

Mr. Santosh Rane was breathing heavily as he reached them. There was a curious gleam in his eyes. He seemed to be quite excited.

Fever

"Hey, Kali, where's your swimsuit?" he demanded, "Go and get it immediately. You will be participating in the competitions!"

For a moment, Kali was too stunned to speak.

The next moment she asked, "But Sir, you know I haven't qualified!"

"No, no, Kali, it's like this, you see," he sounded a bit incoherent, "Hita has come down with severe flu. The doctor won't allow her to compete."

"How terrible for her!" exclaimed Shikha and Kali almost at the same time.

They both liked Hita, she was such a nice girl. Kali knew that she was in class nine, and from Delhi.

"How did she get the flu, Sir?" asked Kali, "You had taken such good care not to let that happen."

"I don't know how she got it," said the coach impatiently, "but now that she has it, she cannot compete. So Kali, you have to take her place. I have already talked to the principal, and he has agreed."

Kali ran over to the dormitory without any more delay, her face shining with excitement. She was going to compete! She would have her chance now to prove herself.

"Oh Lord, thank you for letting me compete," she shot a quick prayer up to God, "But please help Hita overcome her disappointment! Make her well soon, Lord!"

The Dark Mermaid

She went with the coach to the bus carrying the team and, as she was boarding it, Shikha came up to her and informed her that she had changed her mind. She too would be going to watch the competitions!

"Flu or no flu!" she declared defiantly. She was so happy that her friend would be competing.

Sammy sat beside Kali and all through the ride to St. Paul's, flooded her with all sorts of advice.

Kali hardly listened to what he was saying. Her mind was conjuring up vivid images of winning in her events. She imagined herself on the winner's podium, receiving her gold medals to the loud sound of clapping. Kali could see in her mind's eye, the team returning triumphant with the handsome trophy which announced that they were the new Inter School Champions!

CHAPTER 15
THE CHAMPIONSHIPS

As the bus wound its way up the road leading to St. Paul's School, which was some twenty minutes from Mount Hermon, Kali could see that a lot of other buses were also going their way. They waved at the other buses that were carrying students from the other schools taking part in the championships.

They got out of the bus in the parking lot and were greeted by a big burly man with blonde hair. He was the St. Paul's swimming coach. Along with him, was a slim dark woman of around thirty.

"Welcome to St. Paul's," the blonde-haired man boomed in a loud voice, as he shook hands with Mr. Santosh Rane. "Mr. Rane, I want to introduce you to Mrs. Arundhati Roy. She is the swimming coach of St. Helen's School, our partner this year."

"Thanks, Mr. Zavorsky," replied Mr. Rane, "and pleased to meet you, Mrs. Roy."

The Dark Mermaid

They went on up the steps leading to the swimming pool. The pool was festooned all around with colourful paper ribbons. There was a big banner at the far end, proclaiming, 'Welcome to the 7th Inter School Swimming Championships'. Many of the seats around the pool were already occupied by students of various schools. The fifty or so strong contingent from Kali's school took their seats. Kali looked around and saw Reva and Manisha waving at her. She waved back with a big smile.

"Today everybody will notice me," she thought, "and when I win my events, everyone will congratulate me."

Her coach came bustling up to her and said, "Kali, listen to me carefully. I know you are fast in freestyle and backstroke, so I will enter you in both. That means you will have three events. The 50 metres and 100 metres freestyle, and the 100 metres in backstroke."

"What about the relay, Sir?" inquired Kali. "I know I can help the team win."

"Oh yes, Kali, you will also be competing in the girls' 4x100 metres relay," confirmed the coach.

He had made a decision to enter Kali in the relays instead of Romi. He had, no doubt, that his decision was right. Kali was by far the better

The Championships

swimmer. Romi would, of course, be competing in her individual event, the 100 metres breaststroke.

"Kali," the coach said to her as he led her towards the dressing room, "I am sure you'll do well in the heats."

"I will do my best, Sir," said Kali.

The dressing room was packed with other swimmers. Many had already changed into their swimming suits. Kali was glad to see that there were a few dark-complexioned swimmers among the competitors.

"Of course, I must be the darkest," she thought.

Shortly they were all in the pool, warming up for their races. Kali, however, stayed for a few minutes in the dressing room to do some deep breathing exercises. As soon as the room was empty of the other participants, and she was alone, Kali stretched out on the floor, relaxing her whole body.

Her arms limp by her sides, and with legs fully stretched out, she closed her eyes and started to breathe in deeply. She did the breathing exercises for five minutes. After this she jogged in place for a while, her knees pumping up high with each step. Her body now sufficiently warmed up, she started on her stretching routine to limber up her muscles.

The Dark Mermaid

The first heat was the boys' 50-metre freestyle. The students cheered loudly as Sammy won the heats, although Kali could see that the swimmers from Victoria and Dr. Graham's were not far behind, and she guessed that they had only swum as fast as was needed to qualify for the finals.

After this were the heats of the girls' freestyle. Kali proudly walked over to the starting block. Soni was also competing in this event.

"It would be super if we both could qualify!" Soni had enthused in the dressing room.

Now we will know soon enough, thought Kali, taking the ready position. She felt very confident today, her breathing in good stead. The bang of the gun propelled the eight swimmers into the water.

The girl on Kali's left took the lead straightaway. Soni was next. Kali was a little behind the first three, along with the rest. This was the 50 metres. Halfway to the finish Kali had levelled up with the leaders; her body was moving ahead in smooth rhythm. There was no doubt in her mind that she would win, so she did not worry much.

She swam as naturally as she had always done, her concentration on the finish pad. Ten metres from the end, she surged ahead, the familiar frothing wake following her. She touched the end

The Championships

of the pool, slightly ahead of the girls from Dr. Graham's and St. Helen's. Soni finished fourth. The first three would be going to the finals, while Soni, the fourth finisher, would have to wait and see whether the fourth placed in the other heats had better timing than hers. They watched the other heats with interest. At the end of it, Kali was happy that Soni too had qualified by virtue of better timing.

The next event was the butterfly for boys, in which the boys from Victoria and Dr. Graham's came first and second respectively in their group. In the other heats of the same event, Jigmy from Kali's school also managed to qualify, by coming in third behind two boys from St. Paul's and St. Joseph's.

In the next event, Sammy again qualified for the 100 metres freestyle by coming in second. This was followed by the breaststroke, in which Loreto Convent girls did well. Neema from Mount Hermon was eliminated, much to Mr. Rane's disappointment. In the next heat for butterfly, Romi from Mount Hermon just about managed to have herself qualified. In both these events, Dowhill girls were quite good.

Again it was time for Kali to take her position on the starting blocks. It was the 100-metre freestyle, and it was one of the most keenly

The Dark Mermaid

contested of all events. Kali had heard murmurs in the dressing room that St. Helen's and St. Joseph's Convent girls were really very good in this event. Therefore, this time Kali took no chances.

Right from the start she started to take the lead. She was a little wary that starting too fast might leave her with little energy for a good finish, as the race would be over two laps. At the same time, she wanted to take the chance anyway, since she was confident that all the extra stamina-building exercises she had been doing would see her through.

Mr. Santosh Rane was a bit surprised to see Kali start off so quickly.

"I hope she doesn't swim herself out before the finish," he thought warily.

The Mount Hermon supporters in the meanwhile were shouting their lungs off, "Kali! Kali!"

Kali heard her name being chanted and this propelled her all the faster through the water, so that when she turned for the next lap, she saw that the nearest rival was a good metre away.

Seeing that she had such a comfortable lead, Kali slowed down her hectic pace, thinking, "I'd better slow down a little. I must save energy for my backstroke too."

The Championships

At the halfway mark of the lap she saw that the girls from St. Helen's and St. Joseph's were quickly catching up with her.

"Let them catch up," thought Kali, "even if I finish second, I'll qualify anyway."

She was thinking of saving her strength for the backstroke, in which she wanted to do really well, since it was her favourite event.

Ten metres to the finish, the St. Helen's girl overtook her, and Kali decided to let her. But as they neared the last five metres, a little voice inside her commanded, "Come on Kali, after such a good start it's not a good thing to finish second. Go on, swim faster!"

With a sudden burst of energy Kali thrust ahead, her angled arms scything the water rapidly and her feet paddling furiously.

"Well done, Kali!" her coach shouted as she came in ahead of the others.

She pulled herself out of the water and waved triumphantly at the section of the audience where Mount Hermon students were jumping up and down with joy. Kali felt very proud at winning the heats of the glamorous 100-metre freestyle.

"You are as good as you said you were," Sammy said to her as he came up to her, "Congratulations!"

However, Kali was sad to know that her compatriot, Sita, had not qualified.

The Dark Mermaid

In the next hour all the remaining heats were completed, and from her school only Amitava qualified for the breaststroke finals.

The final heat of the day was Kali's favourite event, the 100-metre backstroke. Fortunately, Kali had had a good hour in which to have rest after the tiring 100-metre freestyle. In this time she had mostly done deep breathing exercises. The coach had also had time to give her helpful instructions.

"Don't arch your body too much. And remember to keep your knees under water," he instructed Kali.

The first heat for the backstroke had produced at least three sure finalists, two from Dr. Graham's and one from St. Helen's. As in Soni's case, Sita from Mount Hermon had come in fourth, and would have to await the results of the next heat to know her fate.

Kali saw that there were some tall girls in her group. Of course, it would be to their advantage, Kali knew, but she wasn't very worried. The eight girls took their positions at the edge of the pool, their hands on the rails, their bodies tense under water, their backs arched and facing the opposite end of the pool.

"Ready!" shouted the referee and the girls bunched up their bodies tightly, ready to leap backwards.

The Championships

"Get set!" shouted the referee, his hands holding the pistol high in the air.

"GO!" he shouted, his voice accompanied by the loud bang of the pistol.

All the girls leaped backwards, their bodies stretched to the limit. The tall girls took the lead, as was expected due to their long bodies. However, a few metres on it was Kali, her dark arms flashing in fast efficient half-circles, cutting the water without a splash, who pulled ahead.

Her head was still as a statue's and her legs were going up and down like well-oiled pistons. Kali was the first to flip over at the end of the first lap, the two tall girls following immediately behind. Seeing them so close, Kali became a little tense. Unlike in the other races, she didn't want to be anything but first in the backstroke. Such thoughts did not help and Kali found herself losing her natural rhythm.

"My mind is too tense," she kept thinking, "and this is making my body tense."

Five metres to the finish, Kali found herself following in the wake of the two tall girls, who had now overtaken her. Frustrated at this, Kali willed her arms to move faster, and they did, but now there was really no time to make up the distance between herself and the front runners.

The Dark Mermaid

With vast disappointment, Kali got out of the pool. She had finished third.

"Never mind," her coach consoled her, "at least you qualified for the final."

Kali was not consoled with the coach's words. She wondered if she would be able to win in the finals. She knew that even in the freestyle race, her coming first did not mean that she would win in the finals. Some of her rivals were very good swimmers, and many of them were older than her, as well as stronger.

Since there would be no heats for the relay races, a two-hour lunch break was announced at twelve o'clock.

Lunch was spread out for the teams and their coaches in the huge dining room of the school. Outside the dining hall, Kali saw that there were beautiful flowers all over the well-maintained garden. She reminded herself not to be tempted to take a stroll around the garden; she was reminded only too well of the last time she had admired beautiful flowers in a garden!

The lunch was a hearty one, with lots of meat and bread. Kali took huge helpings of both, she was, to say the least, very, very hungry! Afterwards she took double helpings of the delicious dessert, a plum cake with lots of red cherries and cream.

The Championships

After lunch, the teams went to different corners of the hall to plan strategies with their coaches.

Mr. Rane was crisp and short as he said, "Well team, it looks like we will be having nine swimmers in the finals. Sita, it seems, didn't qualify."

Guiltily, Kali looked over at Sita, she had completely forgotten to check whether her teammate had qualified or not. She had been too disappointed at her own performance. She promised to herself that she would convey her sympathies to Sita soon.

"Kali has done well by qualifying in all her three events, while Sammy has qualified in two. Jigme, Romi, Amitava and Soni will also be in the finals," Mr. Rane informed them. "For the girls' relay I want Kali to be the last to swim. You will have to put in a terrific finish if we are to win the relay, Kali. Likewise, in the boys' relay, I want Sammy to finish, for the same reasons." As an afterthought, he added, "Of course, this doesn't mean that the others in the team will not have to do their bit. Everyone will have to put in extra effort, okay?"

"Right Sir," said Sammy, and the others also echoed his words.

"Good," said the coach, "now, everybody take a rest. You will need it!"

The Dark Mermaid

They trooped back to the dressing room, Kali straggling at the end, her mind deep in thought.

"If we are to become Inter School Champions, I will have to win every one of my events, and I will have to do really well in the relay," she thought to herself. "The coach is depending on me to do the school proud. I can't let the school down!"

CHAPTER 16

A NEW RECORD

The first race of the finals was the 50-metre freestyle for boys. Sammy swam like a champion but was not good enough to be first. The Victoria boy was too good for him and won the race. Sammy came in second, and Dr Graham's third.

In the next race, Kali, to shrieking screams from her schoolmates, won the 50 metres in style, finishing a few feet ahead of the girls from St. Helen's and Dowhills. Mr. Rane was delighted, to say the least. The whole teaching staff of Mount Hermon had come to watch the finals, and the principal himself came over to congratulate Kali, as did a happy Mr. Raj Pradhan.

Soni had finished fifth in the group of seven girls.

In the butterfly for boys, Jigme of Mount Hermon finished third, with a Victoria boy taking the first position and Dr. Graham's boy winning the second position.

The Dark Mermaid

Now, there was an air of expectancy in the audience as the finals of the boys' 100-metre freestyle was announced. Kali went over to Sammy to wish him luck. She could see that he was very tense, and said to him, "Don't be so tense, Sammy, it will only do harm. Just relax and you'll be all right."

"Thanks Kali," Sammy said gratefully, "but, you know it is important that I win this race if we are to have any chance at all of winning the championships."

"I know," Kali said to him encouragingly, "and I know, you will definitely win. Just relax!"

For the first fifty metres Sammy lagged behind the boys from Dr. Graham's and Victoria, but in the next twenty-five, he had overtaken the Dr. Graham's boy and was only an arm's length away from the Victoria swimmer.

"Come on Sammy!" shouted Kali, "Tuck your chin in!"

Five metres to the finish Sammy started to lead, a slim foot separating him from his closest rival. With a determined effort he kept his slim lead, and as he touched the finish pad, he heard a great roar from the Mount Hermon supporters. He had won. It had been really a close thing, but he had won!

In the girls' breaststroke a Dowhill girl came in first, followed by a girl from Dr. Graham's and St. Helens. Romi finished next to last.

A New Record

Then a voice announced over the speakers, "Ladies and Gentlemen, the results so far are as follows: - Victoria and St. Helen's Combined Team is in first position with 2 Gold, 2 Silver and a bronze. In second position is Mount Hermon with 2 Gold, 1 Silver and 1 Bronze. Dowhill has 1 Gold, and 1 Bronze, and is in third place."

There was a big "Hurrah!" from the section of the audience consisting of students from St. Helen's and Victoria High School.

Mr. Santosh Rane sat with Kali in the dressing room and told her, " Kali, you realise that you are our best hope to be Inter School Champions this year. Do your best, girl; we are depending upon you!"

"Don't worry, Sir," responded Kali, a little too confidently.

She was actually feeling quite jittery now. So much was riding on her shoulders! It was probably to conceal her nervousness that she had tried to sound confident.

"Well, Kali, they have announced the race," said the coach, "you'd better go. All the best!"

"Thanks, Coach!" said Kali.

Sammy also came over to wish her luck. As Kali walked over to her starting block, many eyes in the audience were on her. Everyone had noticed how good she had been in the 50 metres. Kali took

The Dark Mermaid

a couple of deep breaths and stretched her arms and legs. She bent down to touch her toes and could feel her hamstrings stretch comfortably. She rolled her shoulders a little and felt strong and sure of herself.

Her two main competitors, the girls from St. Helen's and St. Joseph's Convent, were on either side of her. At the sound of the gun firing, they dived into the water. This time Kali had somehow managed to keep her legs very straight, so that her start was indeed good.

For twenty-five metres, almost all the contestants were level with each other. Near the end of the first lap, the St. Helen's girl had taken a lead of half a metre. The St. Joseph's girl was behind her and Kali was next. They flipped over at the 50-metre mark, and now Kali was only a few feet behind the leader. Ten metres on, Kali was level with the leader, the third girl was an arm's length away.

The Mount Hermon supporters were screaming, "Kali! Kali!"

Kali had taken the lead. Halfway to the end, Kali tucked her chin in, her arms started to move like windmills, and her feet went up and down so rapidly that a bubbly white froth followed her. The St. Helen's girl looked on in dismay. Kali seemed to be accelerating away like a shark.

A New Record

"Come on, Kali!" shouted Mr. Rane, "Keep it up! Keep moving!"

"Buck up Kali! Buck up!" yelled Sammy.

Kali shot a quick glance behind her, she felt truly elated; the nearest rival was a metre and a half away! She was now very close to the finish.

"I might break the record!" the thought went wildly through her head. "I must go faster!"

So Kali accelerated all the more, the thought of breaking the record pushing her to her limits. She touched the finish pad triumphantly and was just getting out of the pool when the announcement boomed out from the speakers, "Ladies and Gentlemen, it's a new record!"

There was a crescendo of cheering from the audience.

"Miss Kali Nepali from Mount Hermon School has set a new record in the Inter School Championships 100-metre freestyle for girls. And it is two seconds under the previous record set by Mae Jong five years ago!"

There was loud cheering from the Mount Hermon supporters. It was a double victory. Mae Jong had also been from Mount Hermon School. How fitting that another Mount Hermon girl should be the one to break her record, unbroken for five long years. Kali was ecstatic. She accepted compliments from her team-mates, coach and

The Dark Mermaid

teachers as modestly as possible. Her mind was now already on the backstroke. She wanted not only to win now, but also to set a new record!

She knew she could do it!

Shikha, along with Reva and Manisha, came to the dressing room and hugged Kali. Even haughty Manisha hugged her, saying, "Oh, Kali, you were wonderful. I am glad to have a friend like you!"

"My friend, Kali, the 100-metre freestyle record holder!" said Reva, "How fantastic!"

Amongst all this, Mr. Rane was a bit cautious. "I hope, Kali, you have not worn yourself out. You have done a magnificent job and we are all very proud of you. But please rest now. You still have other events."

So saying, he shooed away Kali's friends.

The breaststroke for boys was won by Victoria, with St. Augustine coming in second and St. Paul's third. In the girls' butterfly event, the Dowhill girl managed to win by a slim margin over the St. Augustine girl. Loreto came in third.

Now, Victoria and St. Helen's combined team had accumulated 3 Gold, 2 Silver and a Bronze. Mount Hermon also had 3 Gold, 2 Silver and a Bronze, while Dowhill had managed to take third place with 2 Gold and a Bronze. Dr. Graham's Homes, last year's second-placed team, was in fourth place with 2 Silver and 2 Bronze.

A New Record

Now only four more events remained. The boys' and girls' backstroke and the boys' and girls' relays. Mr. Rane was certain that the boys' relay would be won by Victoria High School; their swimmers were all quite good. He didn't fancy the chances of Mount Hermon winning even the Silver.

"And in the boys' backstroke, we don't have a chance either," he thought to himself. "That means, we have to do well in the girls' backstroke and relay."

As he was thinking all this, the principal came over to him and said, "Well, Coach, it seems we have done very well so far."

"That we are, Sir," Mr. Rane agreed, "and it has all been possible mainly due to Kali and Sammy."

"So, do you think we might win the Championship?" asked Mr. D'Souza hopefully.

"It depends on whether Kali does as well as she has done so far, Sir," replied Mr. Rane, "but it's still a very tight thing. She lost in the heats of the backstroke. And in the relay it's very difficult to predict anything."

"Where is she?" Mr. D'Souza searched the room for Kali, their star swimmer.

"There she is," pointed out the coach. Kali was lying prone on the floor in one corner and seemed to be sleeping.

The Dark Mermaid

"Oh, she's resting, is she?" the principal remarked, knowingly.

"Yes, Sir," replied the coach, "but she is also doing some breathing exercises. She told me she does this all the time. I think I will have to make the others also do such exercises in future. It certainly seems to help!"

"Whatever, Coach, whatever," the principal agreed, "As long as we win!"

CHAPTER 17

NECK AND NECK

"The next event is the 100-metre Girl's Backstroke," the announcement brought Kali to her feet. She hopped up and down a few times to get her circulation going. She had been lying down for quite a while. She had thought that she could detect a tiny wheezing in her chest, which became more pronounced as she exhaled.

"Dear God, please help me," she prayed, "thank you for helping so much till now. Please, please, don't let me get asthma now."

In fact, the day's hectic activity had begun to take its toll. Especially the extra effort she had put into breaking the 100-metre freestyle had made her a bit tired. Kali knew that more than anything else, she was feeling mentally tired. The excitement of the races and her exultation at doing better than she expected had made her tremendously upbeat. Her mind went over and over the race in which she

The Dark Mermaid

was now the new record holder, with the result that she couldn't concentrate much on her breathing exercises. Kali tried to calm herself down. She knew that if she could do the deep breathing exercises correctly for a few minutes the wheezing would disappear.

"Kali, they have announced the backstroke," Mr. Rane had come to her side, "Let's go!"

"Sir," requested Kali, "would you please give me a few more minutes please?"

"OK, but you will have to hurry," Mr. Rane replied, "you know they will call the competitors only twice more, and if you don't appear by then, you will be disqualified. So hurry up, OK?"

"I will, Sir," assured Kali.

As soon as he had left, Kali lay down again and forced her mind to go blank. She took a long breath, expanding her abdomen and then her chest, fully, as she held her breath for a count of eight. She exhaled slowly, her chest and her abdomen contracting tightly. She could hear a small wheezing sound as she did so. She repeated the exercise five more times, keeping her mind on her breathing and on nothing else.

By the fourth time, she could detect no wheezing sound. After the fifth, she felt refreshed and ready.

Neck and Neck

She walked out to cheers from her schoolmates and teachers. She waved at them, feeling like a star. As she readied herself in the pool for the start of the backstroke, she felt calm and confident. Her supporters began to chant, "Kali! Kali! Kali!"

"I am a star, a champion," thought Kali proudly, "I mustn't let them down now. I have to win."

The bang from the gun set them off, all the girls springing backwards gracefully. For the first fifty metres there were no clear leaders; all the girls were neck and neck. But as they flipped over at the fifty-metre mark, Kali saw that the girl from St. Helen's was very quick in doing so. Obviously, she must have practised this many times, thought Kali. Because of her quick turn, the St. Helen's girl now took the lead and Kali was right behind her with the others trailing behind.

At the twenty-five-metre mark Kali thought, "Now!" and, gathering all her strength, started to paddle her feet with a furious rhythm, ten beats to one arm stroke. Her arms started to move in fast half circles and her breathing became rapid and shallow. Her body responded by moving through the water more quickly, and Kali saw herself leaving the leader behind. However, she now started to feel a tightness in her chest, and five metres to the finish, she started to wheeze and pant. A few feet from the end she started to falter, her

The Dark Mermaid

pace was slackening and the St. Helen's girl was at her heels.

"Help me Lord!" Kali prayed. Now her chest was burning, her arms, it seemed were not getting enough oxygen, her legs felt heavy. With sheer willpower, Kali ignored the anguish of her burning chest and, with energy that she thought she didn't have, touched the finish line only a few inches ahead of her opponent.

As she wheezed and gasped, taking in great big gulps of air, she heard the wild sound of cheering. She had won her favourite event. Relieved at having won, she didn't mind that she had not created any new record.

"Next time I will," she thought determinedly.

She took some time to climb out of the pool and by then her breathing had become less laborious, although she could still discern a wheezing sound when she breathed out. The St. Helen's girl congratulated her, as did the girl from Dr. Graham's, who had come in third.

Kali, however, didn't hang around long and went into the dressing room to prepare for the relays. Thankfully the boys' backstroke and relay would be next and Kali knew it would be a good half hour before her next event.

The boys' backstroke went to Dr. Graham's, with St. Joseph's in second place, followed by St.

Neck and Neck

Robert's in third place. The boys' relay was won by Victoria School quite comfortably. Dr. Graham's came in second and, surprisingly, the boys of Mount Hermon clinched the bronze. Sammy had swum exceptionally well and in the last fifty metres had caught up and overtaken all but two of the leaders, even though he had started last. It was a tremendous achievement; the coach had complimented him.

"However, now, Kali," said Mr. Rane, "Victoria are ahead with four gold, four silver and a bronze, whereas we are second with four gold, two silver and two bronze. Therefore, I need not stress the importance of winning the girls' relay."

Kali was all too aware of its importance and so were Soni, Neema and Sita, the other three in the team. Kali was very much aware of the fact that she would have to swim extraordinarily fast in order to have their team win.

"Yes, Kali," said the coach, as if reading her thoughts, "you will have to do something special if we are to win. Soni, Sita and Neema, you three will also have to do much better than before."

Since the three girls didn't look too sure of themselves, Kali spoke to them, "Look girls, if we can win this relay we will win the championship, as we will have the most gold medals. Therefore, it's up to each one of us. I can't do it alone. Soni,

The Dark Mermaid

you will be starting and I would suggest that right from the start you go all out. Don't worry about your tiring, as long as you can finish second or even third, it's okay."

"Right Kali," Mr. Rane spoke up, "Sita will be next and she will have to do likewise. Just don't finish among the last three, otherwise the gap will be too great for Kali to make up."

"What about me, Sir," asked Neema. "Do I also do the same thing?"

"Well, more or less the same thing, Neema," said Mr. Rane, "but, in your case, I would like you to concentrate on staying as close as you can to the first three. I am not trying to say that all three of you cannot be in the lead, but since we have seen that the St. Helen's girls have a definite advantage in height and strength, we have to be practical."

"You are right, Sir," said Kali, "I think your plan is very good. If the gap is not too big, I should have a chance to finish first. 100 metres is long enough a distance to catch up, I think."

She, however, didn't think it would be a good idea to point out that 100 metres could also be a long enough distance for there to be big gaps between swimmers.

However, she thought, "I must have more faith in my team mates. I am sure they will do their best."

Neck and Neck

Soni was thinking, "I cannot let the team down. Poor Kali has to do so much; I must be amongst the first three."

"If Kali can be so confident of catching up even when others have taken the lead, why can't I keep the gap between myself and the leaders as narrow as possible? I must do my best," Sita said to herself.

And Neema thought, "Even if I have to burst my lungs, I will see to it that I don't leave too big a distance for Kali to have to make up."

As if reading their thoughts, the coach spoke to them, "Look girls, I know I am asking a lot from you all, but as you know, winning this championship will be a matter of great honour to the whole school. So, we must try our best to win, but please remember that even if we lose I don't want you to think that you have failed. Trying one's best is what is really important."

"But please win, Team, please!" he pleaded silently.

CHAPTER 18

THE GLORY

The four girls trooped out in single file as the last event of the day, the girls' relay, was being announced over the speakers. Since both Victoria/St. Helen's combined team and Mount Hermon had an equal number of gold medals, this last event was proving to be a grand finale to an exciting day of competitions.

If either of the teams won, they would be the new Inter School Champions. If neither won, then Victoria/ St Helen's combined team would take home the championships, since they had more medals overall. Of course, if Mount Hermon were to win, then by virtue of more gold medals, they would become champions. So, it was vital that they win.

"It all depends on me now," thought Kali.

Not only Kali, but almost everybody in the Mount Hermon ranks had the same thought. Kali was on everybody's mind.

The Glory

Reva was thinking, "I am so glad to have her as a friend. I must invite her to our house more often. She looks so athletic!"

"Even though she is dark, she is quite beautiful," Manisha was thinking. "She is tall and so strong-looking. I must ask Mum to throw a party for her."

Ashish, Reva's brother, was also sitting with them. He had joined them in the last hour, just in time to see Kali win the 100 metres in grand style.

"She's a great girl," he was thinking, "I must take her to the movies. It will be nice to be seen with her. Now, everybody knows her. My pals will be jealous of me!" He didn't ask himself why he hadn't done so before.

"She's so dark," he had once said to his mum when she had asked him to show Kali around town, "what will my friends say?"

Anyway, he now blamed Reva's friend, Manisha, for poisoning his mind. She would often remark, "Kali is like the 'before' in those fairness cream advertisements, and I am the 'after'!"

Of course, now Ashish could see that Manisha was chanting, "Kali! Kali!" along with the others, and waving at her as if she was her best friend!

Now the swimmers were ready in their positions. Soni took her place at the starting block. The gun went 'Bang!' and they were off.

The Dark Mermaid

The St. Helen's girl was the first to come out of her dive, with the Dr. Graham's girl behind her. As Soni came out of her dive, she saw that she was four places behind the leader. By the time they had turned at 50 metres, Soni was struggling to keep her fourth position. To Kali, watching keenly, it didn't seem possible that she would be able to do so.

She yelled at the top of her voice, "Keep your chin down, Soni," and Soni heard her above the yelling and screaming of the audience.

She tucked in her chin and put in all her effort to pull herself forward faster by stretching out her arms all the more. At the same time, she put in extra effort to kick her legs faster. Somehow, she managed to take the third place at the finish and as Sita dived in over her, she saw that she had indeed done her job well. Sita was only two places behind the leader.

"Well done Soni!" complimented Kali, pulling her out of the water. Sita was now almost at the other end of the pool and she was still in third place, although the distance between her and the leader was almost a metre and a half. Kali willed her to swim faster, for she knew that if the distance grew bigger then it would be all the more difficult, if not impossible, to make up at the end.

The Glory

She shouted at Sita, "Sita, straighten out your body, move your legs, move your legs!" and Sita too heard her voice above the screaming of hundreds of spectators.

She consciously straightened out her body, gaining more buoyancy, and concentrated on kicking her legs rapidly. Her arms continued their fast scything movements. Ten metres to the end, she was only a metre from the leader, who was a girl from St. Helen's. The girl from Dr. Graham's was an arm's length from her.

"I must keep my place," thought Sita determinedly, and with all her strength, kept up the same strong pace.

When it was time for Neema to dive in, only a metre separated her from the St. Helen's girl who was in the lead, and she was an arm's length away from the second-placed girl, who was from Dr. Graham's. As they raced to the fifty-metre mark, Kali suddenly recognised the St. Helen's girl as the one who was very fast while turning for the next lap. She was now worried that the distance between her and Neema might really widen insurmountably.

Her fears were proven right because, as they came out of their turns, Kali could see that the St. Helen's girl now had more than a metre and a half lead over Neema.

The Dark Mermaid

"I should have warned Neema," Kali blamed herself, "but how was I to know that this girl would be swimming the third lap?"

Kali had assumed that since she was the best swimmer in their team, the St. Helen's coach would save her for the final lap. It was a clever strategy, Kali now guessed, since with a big lead, even if the last swimmer in the team was not as fast, they could still win the race.

"She will have a handicap of almost two metres!" Kali thought, "and that should be enough for anybody!"

Twenty metres to the end, Kali saw Neema getting desperate.

"Oh no, I'm falling far too much behind," Neema was thinking, "I must go faster."

In her desperation, Neema was starting to flail her arms wildly. Her legs were paddling without rhythm. She was trying too hard. She was soon in fourth place.

"Calm down, Neema!" shouted Kali, "Take it easy, don't splash! Cut the water! Cut!"

And Neema too heard Kali's voice above the hundreds of other yelling voices. She stopped flailing her arms, moved them swiftly and surely in rapid movements. Her legs stretched out, her feet kicked the water in quick up and down movements, and she found herself gliding forward smoothly past the girls in front of her. At five metres to the finish, the distance between her and the leader had closed to just one metre.

"Oh Lord, please help me," prayed Kali, as she dived in moments after the girls from St. Helen's and Dr. Graham's. Now the crowd of spectators were on their feet, the excitement was at fever pitch, but Kali did not hear the crescendo of noise. She was in her own world, where the only thing that mattered was overtaking the two girls in front of her.

Her dark arms flashed as they went up and above smoothly and then cut the water neatly. Her feet paddled as fast as they had always done, her chin was tucked well into the water. The positions of the swimmers remained the same for the first fifty metres, but at the turn Kali had shortened the gap. Now she was one place behind the leader, and only by two arm lengths.

She swam like a fish with extra fins, but still couldn't catch up with the leader at the sixty-metre mark. Only forty more metres remained for her to make sure that they won the championships. To make matters worse, she was now beginning to feel the familiar cramping sensation in her chest, her breathing becoming difficult.

She was really overexerting herself now, she had no choice. She put her head under water and

The Dark Mermaid

with a superhuman effort, forced her arms to pull her body faster. She did not care if her heart burst now, she could not, would not, give up!

At the end of the pool, Mr. Rane had a worried furrow on his brow. Something was wrong with his star performer, Kali. Her movements were not as rhythmic as they had been before. It seemed that Kali too was trying too hard, with the result that her whole rhythm was being disturbed.

"Kali, stretch out!" he shouted over the awful din. "Don't over do your strokes. Keep them smooth! Stretch out! Stretch out!"

And Kali heard her coach's voice above the crescendo of noise.

She stretched out her arms while cutting the water, she stretched out her legs so that her body was pulled ahead with renewed force; she stretched out her legs so that her body balance was perfect, which made her efforts more productive. Her legs were now beating more than ten beats for every one arm-stroke, creating a frothy bubble-filled wake.

Five metres to the finish, Kali surged ahead to take the lead. Her breathing was still raspy, her chest burned, her head felt giddy, but she was in front. Now, nobody would be able to overtake her, exulted Mr. Rane.

"She's really gliding now. That's what I call swimming!" he said aloud with great satisfaction.

The Glory

Kali closed her eyes as she touched the finish pad. She took in air in great gulps. She stayed like this for a few moments.

Then as if from afar, she heard her name being called.

"Kali, Kali," it was Mr. Rane, who was reaching out his hand to pull her up.

"Are you all right, Kali," asked Soni worriedly. Kali looked pale and weary.

"I'm okay," she replied, "Just catching my breath."

"We won, Kali," shouted Sita and Neema together, "We are the Inter School Champions!"

"Congratulations, girls!" Mr. Rane said.

Kali got out of the pool and looked up at the audience. Everybody was on their feet, clapping wildly at her marvellous performance. It had been one of the most exciting races they had ever seen. And Kali was their heroine!

Kali closed her eyes and sent a prayer up to God, "Thank you, O Lord! For helping us to win the championships."

To Mr. Rane, she said, "You helped, Sir, I was feeling quite bad at the end. If it wasn't for your instructions, I couldn't have done it."

Mr. Rane was pleased as punch to hear the compliment.

Kali looked up at the medal tally on the scoreboard. It read:

SCHOOL	GOLD	SILVER	BRONZE	TOTAL
1. Mount Hermon	5	2	2	9
2. Victoria/St.Helen's	4	4	1	9
3. Dowhills	2	0	1	3
4. Dr. Graham's Homes	1	3	4	8
5. St Augustine's	0	2	0	2
6. St. Paul's/Loreto Convent	0	0	2	2
7. St. Joseph's/St. Joseph's Convent	0	1	1	2
8. St. Robert's/St. Teresa	0	0	1	1
Total	12	12	12	36

*** NEW RECORD:
100 Metre Freestyle (Girls): KALI NEPALI (Mount Hermon)
****OUTSTANDING SWIMMER OF THE YEAR:***
KALI NEPALI (Mount Hermon)

"CONGRATULATIONS!!!"

The medal-awarding ceremony was like a repeat of the ones she had often seen in her dreams. With four gold medals around her neck, Kali was the most photographed swimmer among all the

The Glory

others. Before the Team Championship Trophy was presented, the announcer informed them that they would now be awarding the prize for the one adjudged Swimmer of the Year.

The crowd chanted as with one voice, "Kali! Kali! Kali!"

"Ladies and Gentlemen," the speakers boomed, "This year the Swimmer of the Year award is presented, by unanimous decision, to Miss Kali Nepali of Mount Hermon School for winning four Gold Medals and for setting a New Inter School Record in the 100 Metre Freestyle for Girls.

To the sound of hundreds of cheers, Kali walked up to the podium to receive the handsome Gold Trophy that was adorned with the figure of a dark mermaid at the top. The Rector of St. Paul's School presented her with the trophy and the Mount Hermon Rector presented her with the cheque for Rs.10000.00.

Kali was ecstatic, how proud her parents would be! She was just walking back when it was announced that Mount Hermon School were the new Inter School Champions and would the coach of the winning school please come forward to receive the prize?

Again to loud cheering, Kali walked over to the podium along with Mr. Rane and the other team mates to receive the glittering two feet tall trophy

The Dark Mermaid

with the inscription '7^(TH) INTER SCHOOL CHAMPIONS' etched neatly on the wooden base.

The principal also came over to the podium to lend a helping hand in holding it high in the air so that everybody could see it. The team hugged each other and the delighted principal shook their hands, clapping each one fondly on the back.

"Well done, Mr. Rane," he said, "you and your team have done it. You have made us all proud!"

"Thank you, Sir," Mr. Rane replied, "but to be honest, this victory was due to the dedication of each team member. And I think everyone will agree that this victory was especially due to Kali."

"Yes, yes, Kali did a marvellous job, we all agree," rejoined the principal, "but the others in the team have also done very well. Well done Kali! Well done Team!"

As the principal was speaking, the loudspeakers came to life again, "Ladies and Gentlemen, there is a special announcement to be made! We are indeed very pleased to inform you that this year's Champion School has been invited to participate in the International Inter School Invitational Championships to be held in Kathmandu, Nepal, this October. This is the first time such a championship is being held in Nepal, and it is being held to commemorate the birth of the new prince, Prince Hridyendra."

The Glory

Kali couldn't believe her ears. The swimmers were murmuring excitedly to each other.

International Championships! and that too to be held in Kathmandu!

"What great news!" Mr. Rane said with great excitement, "This is indeed a pleasant surprise. I wasn't aware of it."

Kali couldn't trust herself to speak. She was just too stunned with the news. In fact, she was delirious with joy! "I'll be competing in front of my mum and dad, and all my friends in Nepal!" she thought, her eyes glistening with delight.

"And I'll be going there as a champion!"